V
PE
GROW
DRUGS

NARCOTICS AND DEVELOPMENT IN THE THIRD WORLD

Michael L Smith
with
Charunee Normita Thongtham
Najma Sadeque
Alfredo Molano Bravo
Roger Rumrrill
Amanda Dávila

PANOS

Published by Panos Publications Ltd
9 White Lion Street
London N1 9PD, UK

British Library Cataloguing in Publishing Data:
Smith, Michael L. et al.
Why people grow drugs: Narcotics and development in the Third World.
I. Title
338.17
ISBN 1-870670 28 0

Funding for *Why people grow drugs* was provided by NORAD, the Norwegian Red Cross, and NOVIB.

Any judgements expressed in this document should not be taken to represent the views of Panos or any of its funding agencies.

The Panos Institute is an information and policy studies institute, dedicated to working in partnership with others towards greater public understanding of sustainable development. Panos has offices in London, Paris and Washington DC.

For more information about the Panos Institute contact:
Juliet Heller, 9 White Lion Street, London N1 9PD.
Steve Lambesis, 1717 Massachusetts Avenue, NW, Suite 301, Washington, DC 20036.

Managing Editor: Olivia Bennett
Production: Sally O'Leary
Picture research: Adrian Evans and Almitra Stanley
Cover design: Graphic Partnership
Cover photograph: Richard Tomkins/The Hutchinson Library
Printed in Great Britain by The Bath Press, Bath, UK.

Contents

Preface   *v*
Acknowledgements   *ix*
Introduction   *xi*

The Gordian Knot: The connection   **1**
between narcotics and development
    Asia, opium and heroin   6
       From Opium to Heroin   10
    The Andes, coca and cocaine   12
       From Coca to Cocaine   14
    Why people grow drugs   18
    The cost of narcotics cropping   21
    Global trends   26
    Responses   29
    Setting the context   34

THAILAND: New Angles in the Golden Triangle   **37**
Fruitful harvest from alternative crops   **39**
    Harvesting 20 years of work   44
    Gaining cooperation   45
    No simple answers   48

PAKISTAN: National Upheavals, Regional
Repercussions   **49**
"God's medicine" bedevilled   **52**
    Opium in central Asia   53
    The watershed year   55
    Accounting for the heroin phenomenon   57
    The frontier provinces and beyond   58

COLOMBIA: How the Coca Cartels Took Root   63

Frontier culture takes to cocaine   65
    Fleeing *La Violencia*   67
    Extending the frontier   68
    "Guaviare gold": the marijuana boom   71
    "White gold": the coca-cocaine boom   72
    The "dirty war"   74

PERU: Watershed in the Andean Amazon   77

The highs and lows of a cocaine economy   79
    Aucayacu: coca's El Dorado   81
    A bar in every front room   85
    Shining Path comes to town   86
    Coca mania   87
      Shining Path: Filling the Void   89

BOLIVIA: Settling Old Scores,
Striking New Bargains   91

Participation, not eradication   93
    Refugees from the Sierra   96
    Unions and markets   97
    Sepes and stompers   99
    Quick profits   102
    A powerful force   103

Institutional Options   105
    Sustainable development and narcotics   107
    The international forum   108
    National government   109
    Local government   110
    Grassroots organisations   110
    Non-government organisations   113
    Taking back the initiative   113

Notes   115
Selected Bibliography   119

Preface

For the past three years, the Panos Institute has watched the thrust of international discussion and policy on narcotics control miss a crucial point. In its current overemphasis on law enforcement, the world community has offered a one-dimensional response to the narcotrafficking problem that has obscured the need to link the issue to viable, sustainable development programmes and institutional reforms in those countries where narcotic crops are grown.

Yet this concern gives rise to a deeper one, which troubles all institutions and people concerned with Third World development. Because rural societies that grow narcotic crops and sell their produce to trafficking organisations reflect extreme conditions of social, political, and economic duress, they constitute a special challenge to what development means as a concept and a goal. They thus become test cases for how to promote and carry out viable, sustainable development models in Third World countries.

When confronting this dilemma of how to break the hold of narcotrafficking through programmes that promote sustainable development, four facets of the problem must be examined:

- narcotics cropping—which is the cultivation of substances banned by national and international law;

- narcotrafficking, with its criminal conspiracy of processing, smuggling and marketing drugs;

- the consumption of banned or controlled substances, including the traditional usage of opiates and coca in rural societies;

- the economic impact of capital through money laundering and investment in other legal or illegal activities.

The effects of these facets vary widely with each substance and in each society or region. Narcotics cropping and the traditional consumption of controlled substances, for example, have their roots in impoverished, pre-industrial societies, yet they have become enmeshed with the twentieth-century phenomenon of narcotrafficking.

These four facets combine to create a systemic problem, which implies that successful responses will have to address all aspects simultaneously. A publication of this length, however, cannot examine all the complexities of the problem. This publication aims to focus more on those issues that have a direct bearing on the developing world.

The five country case studies, each researched and written by a Third World journalist, illustrate how narcotics cropping, trafficking and consumption have affected a specific country. The Washington office of the Panos Institute, which received the original charge to develop the publication, sought to bring forth new voices on the problem. Because of its mandate to encourage and strengthen information centres, journalism and resources in the Americas, as part of an effort to increase information flows from the South to the North, it commissioned reports by journalists in Colombia, Peru, and Bolivia.

As the work advanced, however, the merits became evident of not only including but also beginning with the Asian side of the drug problem. Narcotics cropping in Asia expanded in volume to meet massive demand throughout the continent during the eighteenth and nineteenth centuries. The opium trade thus played a major role in shaping modern-day international affairs and Asian societies. And it was in Asia that the first trafficking organisations came into being. More recently, the spread of increasingly potent drugs within the developing world has been more evident in Asia than in the Andes. And efforts by national governments and international organisations to respond to the problem with crop replacement and rural development programmes have a longer track record in Asia than in the Americas. Thus, examining both Asian and Andean experiences provides a more comprehensive understanding of drug-related issues in the developing world.

Third World journalists add another dimension to their reporting as well. Reading between the lines, one can sense these reporters' concern over the impact of narcotrafficking on their societies, their feeling of impotence at their own governments' inability to respond adequately to the threat, and their discomfort with policies imposed from abroad. These societies are not lacking in the moral resources needed to confront the narcotrafficking threat, as the international media have sometimes portrayed them. But, as the following chapters will make clear, moral resources alone are not enough. The value of these first-hand reports is that they allow the reader to get a more immediate sense of the complexity of the problem in each country.

This publication aims to link the narcotics cropping and trafficking issue with a more fundamental issue—sustainable development—as the most effective means of resolving the root causes of the narcotics problem. Although it does not make any concrete proposals, it does open the door to a more far-reaching discussion of the problem.

Michael L. Smith

Acknowledgements

This publication had a long conception. When the Panos Institute started its operations in 1986, its president, Jon Tinker, saw narcotrafficking as a crucial issue for the developing world. After a diligent search, he matched his concern with that of three European organisations—the Norwegian Red Cross, the Norwegian Agency for Development (NORAD), and NOVIB of the Netherlands—who provided funding to get a narcotics and development information programme under way. Their support and encouragement are greatly appreciated.

Patricia Ardila, the first director of the Narcotics and Development Information Programme at the Panos Institute in Washington, DC, played a primary role in getting the effort off the ground in late 1989. She did the preliminary research, launched a first briefing paper for the Andean drug summit in Cartagena, Colombia, in February 1990, and commissioned the articles for this book. She also co-produced a video, *The Road to Coca,* with the Television Trust for the Environment (TVE) in Britain. Even after leaving Panos, she has made herself available to the programme, unselfishly giving of her knowledge and insight. She also read the final draft of the book and made suggestions to improve it.

A special debt is due to Richard Horovitz, the former director of Panos-Washington. His sensitive leadership and quiet assurance guided the programme through its opening phases. His death in August 1991, after a courageous struggle against the AIDS virus, deprived the Panos staff and his many friends of his personal qualities. This book, in its concern for the underprivileged of the world, has been published in the hope of keeping his memory alive.

In the early phases of the research, Panos Institute consultants Priscilla Annamanthodo (in London) and Marie Thérèse Atallah (in Paris) broadened the base of the information by drawing on

European sources. The five chapter contributors deserve a special thanks because, although they were not acquainted with the Panos Institute personally, they enthusiastically accepted the challenge of writing about a difficult subject. Additional research and writing were done by other journalists in Lebanon, Myanmar, Mexico, and the United States.

The photographs of Peru and Bolivia came from Colombian journalist and photographer Eduardo Márquez, who accompanied Patricia Ardila on an Andean field trip in early 1990. During that trip, Ardila was aided by scores of non-government organisations, grassroots organisations, government officials, and journalists in Colombia, Peru, and Bolivia. Their numbers preclude individual mention.

The translator of the articles that were originally written in Spanish was Charles Roberts. At a crucial point in the production of the book, Jane Gold came to the Panos Institute's assistance as editor of the text. Her professional skills sharpened the focus of the publication and tamed the prose of its multiple authors.

Valuable contributions came from a group of people who read through a preliminary draft of the text and made suggestions to improve the material. Our thanks to Rosemarie Philips, Olivia Bennett, Francisco Sagasit, Ricardo Martín and Diego García Sayán. Professor Richard Crooker of Kutztown University, Pennsylvania, reviewed the manuscript and also supervised the creation of the maps by Michael Hammond, Matthew Parse and Vance Welker.

Special thanks are due to the Panos staff in Washington, who supported me during the writing and editing stages. Executive Director Mencer D. Edwards was unflagging in pushing the programme forward, and Diane McGlynn gave invaluable advice from her knowledge of the early phases of the programme. Other staff members, especially Melissa Rose, Elise Stork and Valerie Barzetti, also contributed their encouragement, experience and comments.

Michael L. Smith

Introduction

Narcotics cropping, trade and consumption has become an international problem of major significance. There are long-term costs to the environment, and to public health, law enforcement and social stability in both producer and consumer countries. The huge sums of money involved distort and corrupt local and regional economies—and in some cases the narcotics industry threatens the development prospects of whole nations.

Since the first attempts to control and restrict the international narcotics trade in 1912, the international community has promoted an approach based on law enforcement, presented in terms suggestive of a moral crusade or war. It has concentrated its efforts on suppressing the supply of narcotics. This has meant that growers have been lumped together with drug traffickers, assumed to be operating from the same motives. Although international policy has now broadened and acknowledged the responsibility of both consumer and producer countries—as journalist Michael L. Smith outlines in his overview chapter "The Gordian Knot"—one legacy of past approaches is that the growers' perspectives have been largely ignored in any discussion of the narcotics issue.

The problems of the peasants who grow coca, poppies and marijuana as an attractive export cash crop must be addressed in the context of development, not from the viewpoint of the police.

This book aims to increase understanding of why people grow drugs. Case studies from Bolivia, Pakistan, Peru, Thailand and Colombia show that farmers cultivate opium poppies and coca shrubs not as part of a criminal conspiracy, but simply in order to survive. Often living in remote, sometimes recently settled, areas which lack government support or public services, they have few options. For a number of reasons, opium and coca are often the best resource to exploit, offering peasants a low-cost entry into the cash economy. Says Don Pablo Sica, a farmer in the Chapare region of Bolivia: "Coca is like our child. It keeps us alive; it helps us send our youngsters to school. Though its price goes up and down, it's still a sure income."

Some farmers or communities cultivate a small amount of narcotics for local or medicinal use, others grow it as a form of insurance against the possible failure of their other, legal crops. Still others cultivate narcotics exclusively. Thus, in the struggle to survive, individuals and groups, "whether they be a hill tribe in the Golden Triangle or a peasant union in the Chapare, Bolivia, make a calculated choice about how deeply they will 'invest' in narcotics crops and how much of their resources they will put into other kinds of activities [1]".

Narcotics cultivation often takes root in isolated areas where government authority is weak. With little or no state support or resources, many growers have developed strong community organisations or built on traditional social structures in order to fill some of the gaps left by the absence of government. These are strengths to be built upon, but narcotics control in the past has concentrated on suppression and eradication—and failed. It ignored the reasons why people grow drugs, which is because it is the most logical response to a set of circumstances which blocks their chances of taking any other route to self-sufficiency. The war against drugs, this book suggests, may ultimately be won not by guns and laws, but by the development of viable alternatives for producer communities.

Today, there is beginning to be more emphasis on the carrot than the stick. Crop substitution is increasingly being promoted, with supporting agricultural services. Nevertheless, if this is not part of a wider rural development programme, prospects of success remain limited. Many growers are suspicious of government initiatives because of the punitive measures of the past; others have been disillusioned by repeatedly broken government promises. One settler in the Ariare River area of Colombia described how the failure of the state to provide transport, access to markets and other facilities, dashed the hopes of many colonisers. "In a year we cleared five hectares....Since the land was virgin, our harvest was healthy and abundant. But what were we to do with so much corn?

How could we get it to market? Carrying it out by foot would have taken another year....By river? Where to? So we had to...leave it to rot....".

Many such families fled deeper into the uncleared land, escaping their debts. In many Latin American and Asian countries, groups of peasants like these, disillusioned and struggling to survive, have proved fertile ground for the narcotics entrepreneurs and their "strange crops". "They landed in Calamar with a small airplane full of coca shoots, took over a large farm, and planted coca. We wondered about all that mystery and just looked on. A few months later, that strange crop was looking mighty nice," recalled one Colombian farmer.

Many of the growers have experienced failed agricultural formulas—rubber, then tobacco, then coffee successively touted as the boom crop of the Amazon frontier, for example—as well unfulfilled promises of services and infrastructure. Others have experienced total neglect. As Bolivian coca grower Don Pablo Sica comments: "We grow coca to survive, because it is the most profitable product. It's not our fault that someone else puts it to poor use. We've been lost and forgotten for 20 years. It took a problem that hurts someone else for people to start talking about us." Hardly surprising then, that many growers are deeply sceptical of government promises to take their interests into account in narcotics substitution programmes. Their instinct is to "stick with a winner as long as it lasts...[as well as to use] narcotics to subsidise legal crops. Peasants thus hedge their bets. That does not mean they are not open to innovation and change but it has to be made reasonable to them [2]".

And nothing will appear "reasonable" to farmers unless it takes account of their experiences and perspectives, is developed with their participation—and is implemented in partnership with organisations in which they have confidence. Given the growers' negative experiences of government and previous narcotics control programmes, another lesson highlighted by this book is the potential importance of non-government organisations (NGOs).

NGOs often work in areas where the state presence is weak, and generally maintain closer relationships with the people with whom they work, and with the existing community organisations. They can assist these groups to get their views and needs across to development and state authorities. They have already proved effective in specific areas such as drug education and rehabilitation; and because they are not associated with the law enforcement and eradication schemes imposed by national and foreign governments, they have far more chance of building a constructive dialogue with grower communities.

Thai journalist Charunee Normita Thongtham writes about a project with growers in the Chiang Mai region: the Royal Northern Project. One key to its relative success is that it had no intention of forcing the hill tribes to plant legal crops but concentrated instead on demonstrating that there were alternatives to poppy cultivation. "The Royal Project has nothing to do with opium repression. Our duty is development....We did ask the police to be lax and give the hill tribes time to stop opium cultivation. Now that the villagers are better informed and know how to plant other crops, the police have become stricter," explains the project manager.

Measured dollar-for-dollar, alternative development schemes will not always be able to fully compensate for the abandonment of narcotics cropping. But the book highlights the fact that, while narcotics cultivation is driven by the need for cash, the growers' perspectives are not confined to economics; they include elements with no monetary value but of extreme significance. These include their demand for greater participation in local government planning and implementation, as well as recognition of their ethnic and regional rights and diversity. Many coca and poppy growers would be willing to see greater self-determination as part of the trade-off in giving up their narcotics crops. If the international drive to reduce the consumption of and trade in narcotics is to be successful, it must take account of the men and women at village level for whom narcotics cultivation is a matter of economic necessity.

Jon Tinker
President
The Panos Institute

The Gordian Knot:
The connection between narcotics and development
by Michael L. Smith

On the isolated forest-covered frontier between Myanmar (formerly Burma) and China, a Wa tribesman deftly puts a curved blade to a green, egg-sized bulb. From each neat incision oozes a white, gummy latex. The next morning, after the latex dries to a brownish black, the tribesman will return to scrape it off. Repeating the action with scores of other poppy plants, the Wa tribesman will then have his cash crop: opium. He will sell it to an opium trader, who visits his hamlet accompanied by an armed escort.

On the other side of the world in another tropical rainforest setting, an Andean farmer picks leaves off a low-growing shrub. He hauls the bales of leaves up the steep, barren slope to his shack and lays them on the hard-baked ground to dry under an equatorial sun. During the following days, he will take the leaves to a secluded site and put them in a soaking pit with water, kerosene, potassium carbonate, and, later, sulphuric acid. The end product from the processing of this harvest of coca leaves will be whitish balls of coca paste, which the grower will then sell to a motorcycle-riding middleman.

To the Burmese tribesman or the Andean peasant, this work may seem no different from what he might do with rice, corn, coffee or cacao. The grower may not even be fully aware of the future uses to which his harvest will be put. Yet, whether in Myanmar, Peru or other source countries such as Afghanistan, Pakistan, Bolivia or Colombia, this work is the first step toward transforming two tropical crops into illegal commodities on the international market: heroin and cocaine.

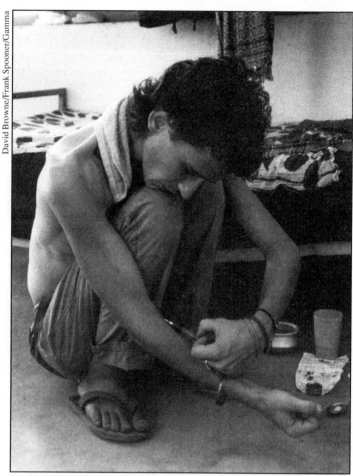

David Browne/Frank Spooner/Gamma

In the journey from growers to consumers, the price of drugs multiplies hundreds of times.

Once the harvest is sold, diverse organisations—guerrilla bands, warlords, criminal syndicates and free-wheeling entrepreneurs —intervene to transform the opium gum into heroin and the coca paste into cocaine. They then smuggle the narcotics out of the source country to consumer markets worldwide. Drug retailers market the drugs on the streets of New York and Amsterdam; some drugs may end up in a Bangkok brothel or in a slum in Rio de Janeiro.

Along this labyrinthine route from tropical field to consumer, the price of narcotics rockets 300-fold. On the way, narcotraffickers amass a fortune worth billions of dollars; the US market alone is estimated at US$100 billion a year. The wealth then buys off judges, prosecutors and politicians. It corrupts police forces and armies, and undermines the legitimacy of governments.

Escalation

In the past decade, narcotrafficking and its associated problems went over a threshold for both Western industrialised nations and the developing world. This, however, means different things to each side. For Europe, the United States and other industrialised countries, narcotrafficking has become a major policy problem on an international scale, involving issues not just of law enforcement but also of public health, criminal justice and international finance, among others. With matters rapidly getting out of hand, a new approach to the problem is needed, one that will require all source and transit countries to apply international law to their own territories in a concerted and systematic effort to reduce narcotics production.

For source countries such as Colombia, Peru, Bolivia, Myanmar and Afghanistan, however, narcotrafficking is a developmental issue with powerful political implications. In the most extreme cases, the ramifications of narcotics cropping and its associated activities have reached dimensions that are undermining the viability of developing societies. To resolve the major drug problems troubling these countries, governments and people will first have to tackle the parallel social, economic and political problems that have fostered narcotics cropping and trafficking and enabled them to flourish.

What has caused the narcotics trade to escalate into an issue of such international significance? First, after the Colombian cartels, which control the cocaine trade, turned the Andean tropics into a major growing area for narcotic crops, cocaine and crack flooded the US market. The amount of money moved by the drug trade grew enormously, as did the US drug consumer base, which expanded to include the white middle class and black urban youths and gave rise to heightened levels of urban violence and crime. This outbreak in the 1980s had immediate political repercussions within the United

States as the US government translated its concerns into foreign policy and made a country's performance on the drug front a litmus test for its status as a law-abiding nation.

Second, the global economy put new instruments into the hands of trafficking organisations. Traffickers no longer confined their smuggling activities to nomadic caravans or mule trains; new means of smuggling drugs and sophisticated financial networks made it easier to engage in trafficking and hide the wealth it brought. Even more troubling, narcotrafficking began to transcend national definitions and policies, outstripping the capacity of any government, including that of the United States, to resolve the problem alone.

Third, in developing countries, urban residents have become heavy drug consumers. In Pakistan, Thailand and Malaysia, the preferred drug is heroin. This shows that developing countries are not immune to the risk of producing a drug-dependent population if a cheap narcotic is readily available. Similarly, Colombia and Brazil have both revealed an increasing appetite for cocaine-based drugs. In Panama, cocaine and even crack is increasingly available and cheap: a pre-packaged dose of crack sells for one US dollar.

In effect, narcotics cropping and trafficking and their associated activities have become a systemic problem. Combating it will require consideration of the complex interplay between supply and demand in both the North (the industrialised countries) and the South. It will require a global approach that applies a variety of flexible strategies to deal with each facet in individual countries and across international boundaries. And it will require making development not an afterthought or a token gesture, but an integral part of any blueprint to reverse the trend.

This approach, however, will first require an understanding of how rural societies have viewed narcotics within their own setting. Rural communities have turned to opium and coca as part of a repertoire of available resources within their limited local environment to ease suffering from illness, hunger and old age. Their association with the narcotics trade has been anchored in their narrow vision of the sale of their crop to a travelling merchant; this vision has included little or no knowledge of how the crop would eventually be used.

Sean Sprague/Panos Pictures

Traditionally, the peoples of the Andes have chewed coca leaves as a mild stimulant and a way of easing hunger and illness.

Growers rarely see how the narcotics trade fits into world commerce and power politics, or the social repercussions from drug-dependent consumers. All they know is that narcotics cropping offers them a low-cost entry into a cash economy because it uses accessible technology and ready markets.

Yet, as the international narcotics trade grows in scale and as developing countries make the transition from pre-industrial, rural societies to modern, urban ones, the full impact of narcotics cropping and trafficking is becoming clearer. Both are wreaking environmental havoc on growing areas in the Andean tropics and Southeast Asia. Narcotics consumption spreads to new user groups, especially in urban centres in both developing and industrialised countries. Narcotrafficking's corrosive power amplifies social violence and political upheaval. The money moved by the trade distorts national economies. Yet these costs are not readily visible to the growers of narcotic crops, who are locked into production out of economic need and limited options.

The root of all evil?

A Pakistani narcotics official asks, "Why should outsiders dictate our choice of crop just because it bothers them? Can we dictate to them the destruction of their alcoholic drinks industry because it has become a menace for us and the rest of the Third World?"

Although Muslims see alcohol as the root of all evil, they have traditionally tolerated opium and hashish. Similarly, peasants in the Andes see their coca leaf as an important part of their culture, and they defend it. Yet despite this cultural defence, peasants would not be planting such large areas in opium and coca unless they were supplying a huge market prohibited by international law and moral codes.

Asia, opium and heroin

Before the twentieth century, the narcotics trade was not in the hands of criminal organisations. An internationally traded commodity like wheat, coffee or tea, opium figured largely in European colonialism in Asia. In the seventeenth century, Portugal and Holland traded in opium as they did in any other spice when they took over inter-Asian maritime commerce from Arab merchants in the Indian Ocean. In the mid-1700s, England gained control of the opium trade and turned it into an elaborate trading monopoly. By joining large-scale opium production in India with new Asian markets, England balanced its regional trade deficit and financed its far-flung Asian colonial regime through tax revenue [1]. It also used opium as a tool of state to open Asian markets, fighting two wars (1839-1842 and 1856-1858) to impose opium commerce on China. The stakes were already high, as China had increased its imports 1,100-fold between 1729 and 1838. The forced introduction of opium into China had important implications.

First, it created a huge consumer market. By 1906, there were 15 million opium addicts and 50 million occasional smokers in China. Opium demand, which reached from the lowly coolie to the imperial mandarin, promoted domestic production, mainly in the southwestern provinces of Sichuan and Yunnan [2]. The volume of production was such that, although China was consuming more than 22,588 tonnes a year, it was importing just 3,000 tonnes, enough to satisfy only 13% of its total domestic consumption. In comparison, 1991 world opium production was no more than 5,000 tonnes a year, discounting legal supply for medicinal uses [3].

Second, the introduction of opium into China created opportunities for Chinese criminal organisations to supply the market. In 1906, in response to greater scientific awareness of the medical repercussions of opium consumption, as well as to an international movement of Christian churches to ban narcotics as "evil", China and Britain agreed to phase out the opium trade, banning production and consumption. Other Western governments soon joined the agreement. China's Imperial Court had already ordered sporadic and sometimes bloody attempts to suppress opium production and consumption [4].

However, these efforts led to a shift from peasant cultivation in accessible river valleys to hill tribe[*] farming in remote areas, moving the crop closer to clandestinity. Moreover, illegalising opium did not stop drug dependency. The situation provided

---

[*]   Internationally, nation or people are the preferred terms when referring to ethnic groups. However, in Southeast and Southwest Asia, the term hill tribe has general acceptance when referring to ethnic groups who live in remote border regions.

Chinese criminal organisations with a golden opportunity: supplied by warlords and their standing armies in southwest China, these gangsters secured a hold on the drug trade, encouraging morphine and heroin as the choice narcotics for consumption. And as Chinese labourers migrated because of overpopulation, lack of employment, and the Chinese civil war (1911-36), they extended opium consumer habits and trafficking networks to Southeast Asia, Europe and elsewhere. Colonial regimes in Southeast Asia also encouraged opium production and consumption as a means of collecting revenue.

Then, following the Communists' triumph in 1949 and using the full range of garrison-state methods at its disposal, Mao Tse-Tung's regime eliminated opium growing in China and made consumers go "cold turkey". Thus, in a short space of time, the country with the largest drug-consuming population in the world practically wiped out its drug problem.

Another related effect of the Chinese Revolution was to shift opium production to northern Southeast Asia—to what came to be called the Golden Triangle: 38 million hectares (150,000 square miles) of rainforest-covered mountains in Laos, Thailand and Myanmar. The region was already criss-crossed by caravan routes for secondary opium smuggling from China to other opium-consuming centres in Southeast Asia. The opium-growing hill tribes of southern China had started moving into the northern reaches of Indochina in the nineteenth century because of ethnic persecution and the need for fresh lands for their slash-and-burn agriculture. This migration now increased due to the upheaval in China. And following the hill tribes were defeated Nationalist Chinese army units who, having often been dependent on warlords who had thrived off the opium trade, now set up their own refining and trafficking networks in northern Myanmar and Thailand. At first, their involvement in the heroin trade was intended to fund an eventual invasion of China to overthrow the Communist regime, but their overseer role in the trade soon became an end in itself.

The Golden Triangle provided optimal environmental, social and political conditions for opium production to take root. The hill tribes had no loyalty to governments in distant capitals from which they were separated not only by distance but also by language,

The Golden Triangle

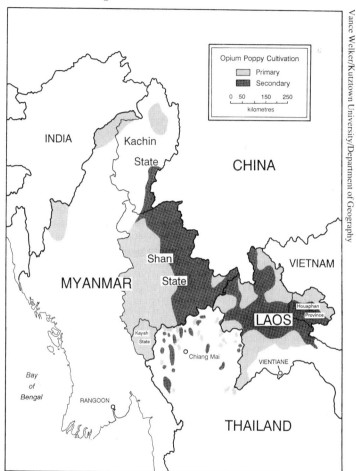

Vance Welker/Kutztown University/Department of Geography

culture and ethnic differences. Nor was there much economic contact between the peripheral regions and the national economies.

Just as importantly, the region was torn by full-scale war in the 1950s and 1960s. The war gave added impetus to the opium-heroin circuit in the region. The complexities of the superpower politics revolving around the war in Vietnam created situations in which first the French colonial government and then the US Central

From Opium to Heroin

Opium (*Papaver somniferum*) grows in a variety of climates, preferring cool temperatures and strong sunlight during its growing season. Opium is Mediterranean in origin and its psychoactive and medicinal properties were studied by physicians in ancient Greece. The plant spread from the Mediterranean throughout the Old World and has also appeared in Mexico, Central America and Colombia.

The opium poppy plant grows about one metre (3-4 feet) tall. About three months after it has been sown, the plant produces a brightly coloured flower. The petals drop to the ground, exposing a green seed pod about the size and shape of an egg. The bulb produces a milky white gum. Farmers collect the opium latex by making a series of shallow, parallel incisions across the bulb's surface with a special curved knife. As the white sap seeps out of the incisions and congeals on the bulb's surface, it changes to a brownish black. The farmer collects the opium by scraping it off the bulb with a flat, blunt knife, sometimes returning for a second or third tapping.

In further refining steps, the opium gum is turned into a more potent extract. This process requires a level of standardisation and quality control. The chemist begins by heating water and dropping in raw opium until it dissolves. By adding ordinary lime, organic waste is precipitated out, leaving the morphine suspended in the chalky white water. Once this is done, there is a second round of heating, in which concentrated ammonia is added to the solution, causing the morphine to solidify and drop to the bottom. The liquid is then filtered through flannel, leaving chunky white kernels of morphine on the cloth. Once dried and packaged for shipment, the morphine usually weighs about a tenth of the weight of the raw opium from which it was extracted.

Then follows a five-step process, in which morphine molecules are chemically bound with acetic acid and refined into heroin. This is a more sophisticated operation requiring heating, filtering and crystallisation. The compound at the end of the process is a fluffy white powder, 80-90% pure, known as No. 4 heroin.

Source: adapted from McCoy, Alfred, *The Politics of Heroin in South-east Asia,* Lawrence Hill Books, Chicago, 1991.

Intelligence Agency (CIA) aided and abetted the Royal Laotian Army and hill tribes, which were actively involved in the heroin trade. Then, in the 1960s, US troops provided a new heroin market and, in 1969, heroin laboratories were introduced into the region, marking an escalation in the productive capacity of Golden Triangle trafficking rings. By 1975, when the last US troops were withdrawn,

Opium Production (in tonnes)

Country	1987	1989	1990
Afghanistan	600	585	415
Iran	300	300	300
Pakistan	205	130	165
Total: Southwest Asia	**1,105**	**1,015**	**880**
Myanmar	835	2,430	2,250
Laos	225	375	275
Thailand	24	50	39
Total: Southeast Asia	**1,084**	**2,855**	**2,564**
Others	53	78	75
Total	**2,242**	**3,948**	**3,520**

Source: *International Narcotics Control Strategy Report*, 1991.

there was a new Asian market of 500,000 heroin users waiting to be supplied [5].

In Myanmar, Communist guerrillas, ethnic insurgents and warlords also got involved in the opium trade in order to finance their fight against the Rangoon government or simply to reap a handsome profit. Unlike the Vietnam war, however, the multiple armed conflicts in Myanmar have continued into the present and have become more deeply enmeshed with the narcotrafficking trade. The situation there has been a shifting game of betrayed alliances, in which traffickers and their money have altered the power balance. In 1979, the US State Department estimated that the Golden Triangle produced about 400 tonnes of opium. By 1990, that figure had zoomed to 2,565 tonnes, mainly due to unbridled production in Myanmar. That country alone could meet the current world demand for opium. In the 1980s, the area under opium went from 20 million hectares (80,000 square miles) to over 46 million hectares (180,000 square miles) and became even more concentrated in the insurrection zones.

The other major opium-growing region in Asia is the Golden Crescent, which stretches across Iran, Afghanistan, and Pakistan (see map on p51). The Kurd, Baluchi and Pashtun ethnic groups have long been poppy growers and smugglers for the large opium-consuming population in Iran. Because national borders were loosely and arbitrarily mapped out, these tribal groups often felt more loyalty to their communities than to central governments, resenting attempts from outside to dictate their crops. An expansion and escalation of narcotrafficking in the region began in 1979 with the Islamic fundamentalist revolution in Iran and the Soviet intervention in Afghanistan. Traditional consumer patterns were disrupted as 4.5 million Afghans became forced migrants to escape the fighting in their homeland. For those who remained, and especially for those who later returned, the breakdown of traditional agricultural and irrigation systems caused by war made tribespeople seek to maximise their earnings by growing opium poppies.

The Andes, coca and cocaine

In the Andes, control of coca-growing areas has been both economically and politically strategic for centuries. During the pre-Columbian era, coca played an important role in the region's barter economy. When the Spanish conquistadors vanquished the Inca empire in 1536, colonial authorities turned coca to their own purposes. As a state-controlled commodity like alcohol, coca was used by the Spanish crown to better exploit its Indian subjects, who were forced to labour in the mines, fields and sweatshops of the viceroyalty. Although the Catholic Church preached against coca consumption as a pernicious, pagan custom, that condemnation did not prevent the Church from collecting a 10% tax on its sale.

After the last of the continent won independence from Spain in 1825, coca continued as a valuable trading product and source of government revenue within local and national economies. Even well into the twentieth century, local feuds and rebellions were fought over control of coca-growing areas. However, unlike opium, which became a major international commodity, coca remained a marginal crop in the Andean economies until the 1980s. Traditionally put to medicinal and dietary use, the primary purpose of the coca plant was to supply the Andean custom of chewing the leaf with burnt lime.

The groundwork for the cocaine explosion of the last decade was laid after the Second World War. Governments in Peru, Bolivia and

Coca-producing areas

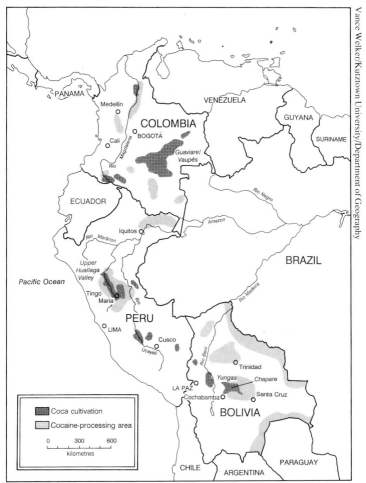

Vance Welker/Kutztown University/Department of Geography

Colombia saw the Andean foothills and Amazon basin as the new open frontier where population growth could be absorbed. Thousands of settlers, many from the impoverished highlands, went into the foothills as pioneers to colonise the virgin land. National governments promised to provide basic infrastructure (roads, irrigation and safe drinking water) and services (education, health and agricultural extension) to make the settlements viable.

From Coca to Cocaine

Coca (*Erythroxylon coca*) is a robust shrub that flourishes on the humid, semi-tropical slopes of the eastern Andes mountains where the sunny climate and acidic soil conditions increase its alkaloid content. Found at 500 to 2,000 metres above sea level and on slopes steeper than 45 degrees, coca plants like heavy rainfall but good drainage. Because the shrub prefers direct sunlight, growers cut down all surrounding foliage, thereby promoting erosion of the fragile soils. The plant reaches maturity in five years, after which growers harvest leaves four or more times annually, depending on weather conditions and their cash needs. They dry the leaves in open, sun-baked yards near their shacks. The growers usually live on site only during the harvest, spending the rest of their time in the towns.

Today, according to US Department of State estimates, Peru cultivates about 120,000 hectares of coca—roughly half the raw leaves needed for the illegal market. Bolivia grows about 50,000 hectares and Colombia about 40,000 hectares but with a low yield. If all the coca produced was transformed completely into cocaine, estimates the State Department, it would yield 700-890 tonnes.

The process of refining coca into cocaine has three stages. The first takes place near the fields. Growers gather their crop and place it in maceration pits: large containers made out of plastic sheeting. The dried leaves are mixed with kerosene and potassium carbonate, which separate the alkaloid from the organic matter. After the waste material is removed, the product is mixed with sulphuric acid. This gooey paste is dried into balls, which form the most common trading article in the Peruvian Amazon foothills: cocaine paste or cocaine sulphate. This initial processing reduces the bulk, cutting down the volume by a factor of 10 and making the product easy to store or transport.

The next stage makes cocaine base: a purer cocaine alkaloid without other

Coca Leaf Production (in tonnes)

Country	1987	1989	1990
Bolivia	79,200	77,600	81,000
Colombia	20,500	33,900	32,100
Peru	191,000	186,300	196,900
Ecuador	400	270	170
Total	291,100	298,070	310,170

Source: *International Narcotics Control Strategy Report,* 1991. These figures are estimates of coca yield and take into account the higher yield per hectare of the crops in Bolivia and Peru where bushes tend to be more mature.

alkaloids mixed in. This process requires more equipment (filters, driers, centrifuges) and chemicals (alcohol, kerosene, sulphuric acid and potassium permanganate). Traffickers set up their labs or "kitchens" in the middle of the rainforest, with portable diesel power generators, plastic sheeting and elaborate logistical support for supplying the chemicals.

Finally, trained chemists turn the cocaine base into cocaine hydrochloride. This stage requires more sophisticated laboratory techniques and industrial volumes of ether so that the semi-processed material can become the crystalline salt necessary for inhaling—the usual form of consumption. Until 1989, this final refining process took place in Colombia, where the cartels enforced their market monopoly, supplying 80% of the world demand for cocaine. The escalation in government repression after the assassination of presidential candidate Luis Carlos Galán in August 1989, however, has forced many of the refining labs to move elsewhere. Bolivia, for instance, now processes 60% of its crop directly into cocaine hydrochloride.

What has held this whole process together has been the Colombian cartels, who have developed their growing areas, distribution networks and marketing skills. They have sought to reduce their dependence on imported precursor chemicals, developing innovative schemes to reduce their consumption of them or recycle them in the refining process. And when challenged, the cartels have responded with ruthless violence.

Cocaine and the Andean Amazon

	Region	Bolivia	Colombia	Peru
Hectares planted in coca	192,840	49,980	27,230	111,630
Tonnes of cocaine paste	1,037	350	109	578
People employed in coca cultivation	433,890	112,455	61,268	260,167
Growers as a percentage of farm workforce	3.7	7.0	1.0	5.9
People economically dependent on coca	964,200	249,900	139,150	578,150
Percentage of total population	1.7	3.8	0.5	2.9
Value of paste to growers in US$ millions	622	210	65	347
Percentage of national agricultural product	6.4	20.9	1.1	12.4
Percentage of retail sales in consumer markets	0.9	0.9	0.9	0.9

Source: from de Rementería, Ibán, *Boletin de la Comisión Andina de Juristas,* No 26, September 1990, p30, citing US Department of State and World Bank figures for 1989.

Over the next few decades, the peasants and colonisers of the Upper Huallaga Valley in Peru and the Chapare and Yungas regions in Bolivia (see map on p13) heard government agricultural promoters successively tout rubber, tobacco, tea, coffee, cacao, rice and maize as the next boom crop on the Amazon frontier. Yet each time, after an initial spurt of activity, the dream crop failed to live up to claims. In now classic boom-bust cycles, colonisers stumbled back to subsistence farming and a meagre existence made worse by the concomitant failure of the national governments to fulfil their commitment for infrastructure and services.

In the mid-1970s, after scores of mainstream agricultural development formulas had failed, Colombian traffickers began to appear in the settlement areas. With an efficiency unencumbered by government bureaucracy or regulations, they brought in coca seeds, set up demonstration plots, provided venture capital and guaranteed purchase of the harvest. The cartels also diversified their coca suppliers by introducing coca into the Colombian Amazon, even though growing conditions there did not permit a high yield or good alkaloid content. From that time and through most of the 1980s, coca acreage grew by 10% a year. Despite price variations, which momentarily dampened grower enthusiasm for the crop, the boom was riding on the back of US demand, the ingenious trafficking and processing systems set up by the cartels, and the half-hearted attempts by national governments to control the trade.

For three Andean countries—Colombia, Peru and Bolivia—the 1980s could be called "the cocaine decade" because of the huge impact the white powder has had on their social, economic and political make-up. The repercussions, however, have reached beyond these three countries to the whole of South America and indeed the entire western hemisphere. Cocaine consumption is responsible for the spiralling street crime in Brazil, having given rise to retailing gangs that rule the *favelas* (slums) of São Paulo and Rio de Janeiro [6]. Because of their proximity to Colombia and their inability to control the traffickers' financial operations, both Ecuador and Venezuela have become preferred centres for money laundering [7]. Even Argentina, at the other end of the continent, has seen a marked increase in trafficking as traffickers exploit its diverse trade links with Europe [8].

Caribbean island nations—whether conservative, pro-business governments such as the Bahamas or socialist strongholds such as Cuba—have found themselves used as way-stations en route to consumer markets. Mexico, which shares an extended frontier with the United States and had already been drawn into the narcotics trade because it grows heroin and marijuana, has become a major transhipment country, especially after the United States stepped up interdiction efforts in Florida and the Caribbean in the mid-1980s. Central American countries have also become refuelling and transshipment points on the midnight routes to US consumers. And the United States has become the main consumer market for cocaine at an estimated volume of between US$76 billion and US$180 billion at the retail level. In just one offshoot of the problem, according to a 1991 report of the Inter-American Commission on Drug Policy: "Over 300,000 babies are born each year in the United States who have been exposed to illicit drugs, including cocaine and its especially harmful derivative, crack [9]."

Clearly, the historical heritage of narcotics has given both opium and coca a medicinal, cultural and social legitimacy within the rural societies that grow them. Opium has been an integral part of Asian society for more than three centuries; even a modern drug like heroin has been present since the early 1920s. Demand for the drug by Europe and the United States has remained relatively constant throughout the past 20 years. Where consumption has increased is in developing countries such as Pakistan, Thailand, Myanmar and Malaysia. And although the primary supplier of the heroin trade has shifted over the past four decades from Turkey to Iran to Myanmar, the opium poppy's well-established growing areas and relatively stable consumer market have ensured that the supply of heroin depends only on weather conditions, comparative advantages of one growing region over another, and other variables—for example, tougher interdiction, political disruption—rather than on the vagaries of social trends.

Cocaine trafficking, by contrast, is a recent phenomenon. Just two decades ago, cocaine was an exotic drug largely confined to the US entertainment business. Its huge growth in the US market in the 1980s came from a social acceptance of recreational drug use and the intensification of poverty in inner cities. Today, the marketing capacity of the Colombian cartels has outstripped the ability of law enforcement agencies to stop the wholesale and retail selling of cocaine. However, the glut of coca leaves in Andean growing regions and the low prices since 1990 point toward a shift to a more stable, mature market like that for opium, one in which growers become sensitive to price and the process is dictated not by steadily rising demand but by a more complex formula containing political, financial and legal factors.

Why people grow drugs

Why do growers of narcotic crops participate in this process? Do people in Afghanistan and Myanmar grow poppies because they are criminal by nature? Do peasants in the Andean tropics plant coca as part of a sinister conspiracy to poison the Western world?

Growers have become involved in narcotics cropping because they face a set of circumstances that has blocked their chances of finding a more secure place in their national societies—or even of surviving. They are as much hostages of the drug trade as is the junkie on New York's Times Square or the Colombian judge with a death threat hanging over his head from the cocaine cartels. Although the growers receive an attractive price for their crop, it is only a fraction of what traffickers receive for delivering the drugs to consumers. Growers also bear the burden of cultivating an illegal crop. Locked into a production system that effectively prevents them from developing their full potential within national societies, they face the prospect of losing their land, their belongings and even their rights as citizens. In effect, they have become sharecroppers to the traffickers.

In the cases of both the opium-heroin and coca-cocaine circuits, the growers are in a state of flux between a traditional, rural, community-oriented society and a modern, urban, market-oriented one. For the advantages of better living standards and public education there is a price to be paid: becoming part of a wage-earning labour force in an industrialised society where the traditional support of community institutions is absent. The transition from one kind of society to another is not an easy one, and past experience has figured as heavily as present circumstances

Opium cultivation in Thailand. For many farmers, narcotics are the only crops which make it possible for them to enter the cash economy.

in forming the choices growers made in their efforts to adapt. For those who live where conditions are favourable for narcotics cropping (the right soil and climate combined with absence of government), such crops offer the farmers a way to adapt their old lifestyle to the modern world. Thus, the bonds that link growers to drug merchants are often grounded in personal acquaintance, ethnic ties and cultural resistance to central authority.

Beyond the initial appeal, there are short-term gains that attract farmers to this way of earning a living. Most analysis of narcotics cropping has focused on the price factor: coca and opium fetch better prices than legal crops, giving peasants ample motive to grow them. However, some analysts say that opium is not always the most profitable crop because it is labour-intensive. Moreover, the high fluctuation of opium acreage in Asia seems to indicate that growers are highly responsive to price swings.

Yet many farmers have cast their lot with narcotics cropping for reasons that go beyond purely comparative pricing:

- Opium and coca are non-perishable low-bulk crops, which means they are easily stored and transported. Opium growers collect a latex or gum by slicing the flower's bulb, a natural bulk-reduction process. The initial processing of coca into cocaine reduces a volume of 10 kg of coca leaf to 1 kg of cocaine.

- Small-scale production of 1-3 hectares (or even less in the case of opium because the crop requires 20 times more labour during harvest) is enough to maintain a single-family household with seasonal hired help. Thus, smallholdings become economically viable. Furthermore, narcotic crops subsidise legal crops that would not be grown otherwise. Farmers thus hedge their bets against crop failure, a traditional means of spreading risk in peasant economies.

- By and large, farming techniques for narcotic crops are familiar to most peasants, who draw on their own customs. Small-scale use of fertilisers, herbicides and pesticides do bring higher yields, but the new techniques are spread by both word of mouth and example, not by "outsider" agronomists or extension workers.

- Growers may engage in initial processing, which adds value to their crops and secures an increased profit margin for themselves. In the case of coca, market dynamics push coca growers toward initial processing, especially as overproduction pushes prices down.

- Narcotic crops require only low start-up costs, so peasants do not need a sizable capital base to start production. Traffickers make advance payments, and day labourers can save enough money to start up. Then, with their first mature crop, the labourers can farm independently.

- Finally, there is market access. Despite the isolation of producer areas, narcotic crops do not depend on the precarious state of the highways or other transport systems to get to market. Not only are the crops non-perishable, but the market is identifiable and constant, even during war or natural disasters when farmers may not be able to get other crops to market.

Clearly, in enlisting farmers into the low end of the narcotics business, the drug networks have successfully used some of the dilemmas and bottlenecks of underdevelopment to their advantage.

In effect, they have produced, by design or chance, packages of technology ideally suited to undercapitalised farming units in rural economies.

There is also a political aspect that increases the appeal of narcotics cropping for growers. Many of the ethnic groups have always enjoyed a high degree of autonomy from central authority. Historically, in southern China and northern Southeast Asia, most hill tribes resisted taxation and other forms of control by lowlanders. In other parts of Asia, autonomy is a heritage from colonial times; the British, for instance, allowed the hill tribes of Pakistan and the Shan States of Myanmar to continue with their own governments, provided they swore allegiance to the Crown. As a result, when central governments try to assert their control, this intrusion creates friction, especially because these governments are often predominantly in the hands of antagonistic ethnic groups. In the Andes, this autonomy has developed from the self-reliance of the growers' associations, which have had to assume basic functions that would ordinarily be provided by the state. Any attempt by the government to exert control would mean the farmers having to forgo their illicit activities.

Finally, in some cases, growers may have no choice but to grow narcotic crops because armed groups—guerrillas, warlords or traffickers—threaten them with force if they do not. Local governments may even charge taxes in narcotic crops.

The cost of narcotics cropping

Before any assessment of narcotics cropping as a productive activity that is sustainable in developing economies can be done, certain long-term costs must be taken into account. They include damage to public health and social stability, and the corrupting and distorting effects of the associated illegal and financial activities.

Environmental impact

Traditional slash-and-burn agricultural techniques in the jungles of Southeast Asia and the Andes were ecologically benign when isolated tribes and growers used them on small plots of land scattered around the rainforest. However, over the past few decades, as population density has increased on these agriculturally marginal

As the demand for drugs has increased, so have environmental costs.
Widespread clearing of the steep slopes on which coca thrives has
accelerated soil erosion.

and fragile lands, such practices have become extremely damaging
to the tropical rainforest environment. Opium growers farm the
same fields for two or three years, depleting the soil of nutrients,
and then they repeat the process, clearing new land for more crops.

In the eastern Andean foothills, fresh influxes of people attracted
by narcotics cropping denude forest hillsides and step up the
depredation of the environment [10]. Instead of growing small plots
to supply traditional coca leaf consumption, as in the past, farmers
now grow coca as their main cash crop and do not use adequate
farming techniques for the tropical soil. Because coca bushes
require good drainage, peasants plant them on steep slopes—which
are the most vulnerable part of the Amazon soil system.

Farmers have also started using modern farming technologies
—herbicides, pesticides and fertilisers—to increase profits. But
because narcotics cropping is outside the legal system, the farmers
rarely receive technical help over the proper use of agricultural
chemicals or alternative farming systems. Thus, in the late 1980s,
Peru's Upper Huallaga Valley had the highest per capita
consumption of agricultural chemicals in the country.

In addition, drug processing labs dump their untreated chemical waste into streams. According to one calculation, for each hectare of coca, the result of initial processing are two tonnes of such chemicals as kerosene, ammonia and sulphuric acid dumped into the water; such pollution has killed off fish in the Huallaga River. In Asia, the chemical residue from heroin refining includes ammonium chloride, hydrochloride acid, acetic anhydride and sodium carbonate [11].

Finally, the intensive settlement pattern, combined with deforestation, poor watershed management and pollution, threatens the biodiversity of the Amazon and Southeast Asian regions. Narcotics cropping, which could wipe out indigenous species of flora and fauna, has even reached into Peruvian parks and nature reserves.

Public health and drug consumption

Some countries in the developing world have seen a dramatic rise in drug consumption, especially of so-called hard drugs such as heroin. There has been little research, however, into the causes of this epidemic in developing countries. According to development writer André McNicoll,

> What seems to be taking place is a Westernization of drug-taking patterns, a process facilitated by the rapid erosion of traditional controls over intoxication. There is a demographic factor that must be considered when accounting for shifts in drug-taking patterns....The Third World is undergoing rapid industrialization and urbanization, as well as experiencing a reduced mortality rate with a concomitant increase in the number of young people in the population, all factors thought by many to be intimately linked to high drug abuse rates [12].

In countries that cannot even provide minimum preventive health care for infants, drug consumption places a serious burden on society. In source countries, the risk is especially high because of the availability of cheap, dangerous drugs. The technology required to produce the most refined narcotics is no longer in the exclusive domain of international syndicates but can be used by local traffickers to increase their profits. As heroin traffickers put labs closer to their raw material sources, they increase the likelihood of heroin use all along trade routes. The government of Sri Lanka acknowledges 50,000 heroin users; in Malaysia, there are 145,000.

The Pakistan government reports 1.1 million heroin consumers, 43% of whom are between the ages of 16 and 20. Drug consumption has hit hardest among young urban males who are predominantly unemployed, better educated and less traditional than the population as a whole [13].

In countries such as Myanmar and Thailand, consumers are starting to inject heroin instead of smoking it. And since one way that the human immunodeficiency virus (HIV) is spread is through contaminated blood, the growth of needle-based consumption adds another serious health risk [14].

Even traditional forms of opium consumption can have devastating results. Among the Golden Triangle hill tribes, if the head of a family becomes dependent on opium, it can destroy the family's productive capacity. Dependency rates in some hill tribes can range between 6% and 38% of all villagers aged 10 years or older. Opium consumption can also lead to declining standards of hygiene, health, nutrition and labour productivity. Anthropologists report cases of households and communities breaking down and of children being sold into bondage [15].

In the Andean regions, cocaine consumption has been isolated in small pockets. A more serious threat is the smoking of a mixture of coca paste and tobacco: *pitillo* in Peru and Bolivia, *basuco* in Colombia. This substance causes quick addiction and permanent brain damage because of the high concentration of chemical impurities remaining in the drug. Use has been concentrated among unemployed youths and other marginalised sectors. Colombia may have as many as 500,000 *basuco* smokers [16].

Drug-related crime and violence

A leitmotiv runs along the drug routes in the developing world: the Kalashnikov automatic assault rifle, or AK-47. The carriers of the guns may differ politically, ethnically or racially, but narcotrafficking—whether in the Golden Crescent or in the Upper Huallaga Valley, in Lebanon or in Laos—provides a common medium in which users of violence can breed and prosper. For that matter, Los Angeles and Washington, DC, can also attest to the violent impact of drugs, although the weapons used there may be of a different calibre.

Narcotrafficking can corrode the legitimacy of government through corruption and the breakdown of shared values and consensus. In Colombia, the cartels have struck at those professions that, by focusing on and enforcing social values, dare to challenge the cartels' pragmatic interests. During the 1980s, 45 judges and 42 journalists were assassinated. For many members of the courts and the press, self-censorship became the only way out of the dilemma of confronting the cartels.

Economics

Drug revenues may seem to provide a windfall to a producer country's central bankers in times of financial hardship, high debt burdens and structural adjustment policies, but the full consequences of a drug-fuelled economy erases any short-term gain. Colombia weathered the Latin American debt crisis practically unscathed, thanks to conservative financial management and a blind eye to the money flowing into its international reserves from trafficking. Peru and Bolivia have also been able to ward off economic collapse because they have hard currency from the drug trade as a last resort. Yet there are other ways of assessing the financial and economic impact of the drug trade.

Economic studies have shown that narcotraffickers leave only a small share of their profits in source countries. But even that small return can distort economic systems. The foreign earnings from narcotrafficking usually translate into an overvaluing of local currencies by 10-20% [17]. This makes it hard for legitimate exporters to recover their costs. Narcotrafficking also makes a country less attractive for foreign investment. Traffickers do not pay taxes, either, thus depriving governments of revenue.

It becomes extremely difficult to carry out serious development work while narcotrafficking is present, because it stacks the cards against legitimate enterprises. For one thing, production factors are distorted. For example, labour wages in coca-growing areas can be up to four times greater than they are elsewhere, making labour-intensive businesses uncompetitive. Second, narcotrafficking often ends up strengthening the merchants, those intermediate links in the market chain who represent conservative political concerns and thus obstruct more equitable development in rural areas. These commercial interests benefit most from trafficking cash flows because rural peasants have money to buy goods and thus become less reliant on subsistence farming. Merchants then jack up prices because of the overheated local economy created by trafficking. Moreover, the urban merchants are often in a position to "invest" in the drug trade by buying up harvests, processing them, and then selling them to international traffickers. This bottleneck in rural markets in developing countries is why any attempt at alternative development strategy must introduce major changes in the marketing of tropical produce [18].

Finally, the laundering of narcodollars can distort the local economies in other ways. To disguise their illegal profits, traffickers set up "front" companies as covers for their operations or as "loss leaders". Many lumbering operations in the Peruvian Amazon got their start-up capital from the narcotraffickers; this led to the irrational exploitation of natural resources. Similarly, large-scale lumbering concerns in virgin forests of Myanmar today are partially encouraged by parallel trafficking operations.

Global trends

Its long-term costs notwithstanding, narcotics cropping is currently a thriving enterprise. This success can be attributed to several factors that have assisted the expansion of drug-producing and marketing networks worldwide.

Technology

The introduction of the tobacco pipe in seventeenth-century Asia paved the way for the mass consumption and smoking of opium. The twentieth-century equivalent is the hypodermic needle, which made possible a new generation of more potent drugs. Although refined narcotics have been around since the late nineteenth century and their marketing and use had become linked to criminal organisations by the 1920s, their real impact on developing countries came after 1970. At that time, the technology, skills, precursor chemicals and equipment needed to produce narcotics became widespread in or near the source countries. Other less obvious technological changes have also had an influence. The outboard motor and the light aircraft, for example, are two innovations that made trafficking more viable in remote regions.

Trade

Another boon was the huge growth of world trade following the Second World War. No longer isolated from international markets, the source countries were now claiming an increasing share of commerce. Between 1965 and 1985, the developing countries' share of international trade of manufactured goods grew by 250% [19]. As both the volume and the diversity of developing countries' commerce increased, smugglers had more opportunities to get their contraband past customs agents and narcotics police, to develop alternative routes and to diversify their transport methods.

Crisis in governance

The optimism that came to the developing world after the Second World War has petered out in the harsh realities of a highly competitive world market with limited resources. In Asia, the break-up of colonial regimes has not created viable governments in all the newly independent countries. Often, the national boundaries inherited from the colonial past have not encompassed integrated societies. In Myanmar, Laos, Afghanistan and Pakistan, the ethnic divisions and the absence of integrating institutions have prevented governments from being truly representative.

Heldur Netocny/Panos Pictures

Shan smugglers on their way from Myanmar into Thai territory.

Even in Latin America, where nationhood dates back almost two centuries, national governments are operating under severe stress because of the debt crisis, diminishing resources brought on by austerity measures and the weaknesses of democratic institutions. In addition, while the cocaine trade was taking root in South America in the 1980s, eight authoritarian, military regimes in the region gave way to freely elected governments, leaving those democratic governments with little time to consolidate. On another level, Third World governments have not been able to offer models of economic development.

The guerrilla insurgencies that have plagued Myanmar, Afghanistan, Peru and Colombia are signs that national governments have lost the confidence of a portion of their population. And narcotics cropping and trafficking have sprung up where the state has been weakest in both asserting authority and meeting needs. These areas have typically been located in remote regions, where it is difficult for governments to provide even the most basic services. For governments to integrate these border regions into national societies, they must gain acceptance from the local population and develop institutions that can set goals and policies for attaining them. The question of governance is primarily a factor of viability, efficiency and legitimacy.

Under these conditions, there is no "quick fix" for narcotics cropping or trafficking, either through law enforcement or through provision of alternative economic activities. Indeed, governments will have to lay the foundation for national development and institution building before they can provide specific responses to the narcotics issue.

From smugglers to international entrepreneurs

Finally, the current situation would not have been possible without the emergence of new trafficking organisations—those with skills, resources and vision. The *de facto* narcotics monopoly of the European or Chinese criminal organisations broke down as new groups entered into the narcotics business. With more players in the drug trade, competition to capture and expand markets increased. The most spectacular protagonists in this boom industry have been the Colombian cartels, who went from being provincial smugglers to sophisticated, world-class entrepreneurs in less than a decade.

Although efforts at interdiction have intensified, they only result in inefficient traffickers being weeded out, thereby increasing the opportunities for those who survive. For their part, the powerful cartels and syndicates are adapting to interdiction efforts by increasing the scale and complexity of their networks. They also have new markets available in Europe, especially in the former Socialist bloc countries. Although totalitarian restraints have been removed in Eastern Europe, no new government can deliver immediately on higher living standards. Thus these nations, too, are easy targets for expanded narcotrafficking activities.

Responses

In February 1990, US President George Bush and the three Andean presidents at the time—Virgilio Barco of Colombia, Alan García of Peru, and Jaime Paz of Bolivia—gathered in Cartagena, Colombia, to mark a breakthrough in the regional strategy against narcotrafficking. Source and consumer countries shared a common interest in working together in a multi-front effort, and there was a tacit acceptance of co-responsibility. The Andean heads of state saw this recognition as an opening for them to broaden the agenda to include other issues besides law enforcement, such as trade and development.

A few days before that summit, the Andean Commission of Jurists, a non-profit, non-government organisation specialising in human rights, organised a conference on narcotrafficking in Peru. It brought together a varied group of participants ranging from Bolivian and Peruvian coca growers to Colombian journalists under death threats from the Medellín cartel, human rights advocates, anti-narcotics police and environmentalists. Representatives from the European Community and the United Nations also attended.

The US embassy mobilised its staff to corner individuals at the seminar and expound on Washington's fresh commitment of new resources and political will. In their efforts to win points, US officials had to lobby and cajole not just bureaucrats and police authorities from producing countries, but also new participants who were entering the public debate for the first time, having missed the early phases of discussion. These newcomers, convinced of different cultural, political and economic realities, pushed their own agendas and priorities. Participants saw the narcotics issue within their national setting and were limited in their ability to see how it affected places outside that context. In the seminar discussions, it often seemed that Bolivian coca growers had more acrimonious and deeply rooted disputes with their own government than they had with the United States. Other participants saw US anti-narcotics policy as an extension of 50 years of US interventionism in Latin America.

On the second day, after participating in a heated three-hour debate, veteran US diplomat Mark Dion looked out on an audience of 120 people and said with scolding bluntness:

> I am depressed [that] after five years of joint efforts with many of the governments of the people in this room to overcome what had been a sterile exchange of accusations and insults....I thought we had reached a stage in which we could begin to confront a joint problem [and], through a long, complex negotiation, arrive at agreements. What I have heard here this morning in this meeting has been the bitter criticism from four or five years ago [20].

That evening, out of frustration, the US embassy decided to withdraw all but one of its staff from the meeting.

What Dion and embassy colleagues failed to realise was that the US government had become a victim of its own success. It had put narcotics cropping and trafficking on the political agenda internationally and had convinced international organisations and governments, as well as world and national leaders, opinion-makers and publics, that narcotrafficking is a top priority.

Since the Hague Convention of 1912, which included the first attempts to control and restrict the international narcotics trade, the United States has played a pre-eminent role in pushing an approach focused on supply countries and based on law enforcement measures to stop the flow of drugs across borders. "For many decades, the US has always regarded the non-medical use of opiates as a great moral and social evil and seen itself as a 'victim country'," writes André McNicoll. "Since [1909], Washington's influence has risen and national drug policies have been woven into overall policy [21]." Washington has shaped treatises and placed US citizens in key positions in international narcotics control organisations to ensure compliance, at least with the letter of the law.

This dominance of the issue has made it look as if drugs were exclusively a US problem and has made Third World countries suspect US intentions. At the same time, the United States has sent its own crossed signals to other countries. Just as the CIA had tolerated heroin trafficking in Southeast Asia during the Vietnam war, Washington turned a blind eye on the direct involvement of the US-sponsored *mujahedin* (freedom fighters) in Afghanistan's heroin trade because it was interested in undermining the Communist-led government in Kabul. In addition, Washington has persuaded the governments of both Bolivia and Peru to sign debt repayment agreements with the International Monetary Fund, although the only way these countries can meet repayment schedules is by tapping black market dollars from the drug trade.

The arrival of cocaine on the US scene in the late 1970s and early 1980s, bringing with it drug-spurred urban crime, against which the police proved ineffectual, as well as the broadening social consequences of drug consumption, made the previous heroin-fuelled concern seem insignificant. By the mid-1980s, 50-85% of those persons arrested in major cities tested positive for drug use. Moreover, there were about 2.2 million hard-core drug users in the country, according to a 1991 US Senate report [22]. At times, near hysteria in the news coverage fanned the flames. And because, in a reversal of the usual patterns of drug consumption, the cocaine plague first took hold not in the black inner cities but in the white middle-class suburbs, the re-election hopes of many US congressmen began to hinge on how tough Congress and the administration could be on the drug issue.

This political momentum reached its peak in 1989, when President Bush unveiled the National Drug Control Strategy, otherwise known as the War on Drugs. Often couched in political terms that are suggestive of a moral crusade, this strategy is set in the framework of a national security concern that renders it more reassuring to the US public and Congress than useful in explaining Washington's drug policy abroad. Still, it is the most comprehensive policy statement the US government has produced in 90 years. And it shows the extent to which the US drug policy has evolved and broadened its scope over the past decade.

In a major change, the Bush administration has admitted that the narcotrafficking problem encompasses a co-responsibility between consumer and producer countries. This is an improvement after the mutual recriminations of the preceding years. The administration has also recognised that a prerequisite to a viable anti-narcotics policy is an economic development component. It has also intensified its efforts to reduce US consumer demand, although far more of the burden of this responsibility ends up falling on cash-strapped local and state governments. As always, the interdiction and drug intelligence role of US policy remains in the foreground.

In a more controversial vein, the Bush administration has also funded more aggressive involvement, especially in the Andean region. This initiative has sparked sharp criticism from human rights advocates and other administration critics, who believe militarisation in the anti-narcotics strategy weakens efforts in Latin American and Asian countries to become more democratic. This is because the military has been the least cooperative group in accepting civilian supervision and because, out of institutional rivalry, a military command prevents a professional police force from developing expertise and leadership. This is what happened in Peru and Bolivia [23].

However, for the US narcotics control policy to be more effective internationally, it needs to enlist not only the active support of the source countries but also the backing of other countries, whether they have a large drug consumer population, are transhipment points or serve as money-laundering centres.

European governments have also awakened to the need to present a more concerted approach to the drug problem. According to Interpol figures, cocaine seizures in Europe for 1990 were 15,000 kg, a 10-fold increase over 1986. Spain and the Netherlands were the gateways for Colombian smuggling operations [24].

Most governments, however, have resisted following the US policy line, with its emphasis on law enforcement and its insistence on seeing narcotics as a national security threat, and are trying to generate a joint international narcotics policy with a development component, through the European Commission. However, given that the break-up of the Socialist bloc has offered traffickers an

Paul-Henry Versele/Gamma

Cocaine seized by Belgian customs en route to Amsterdam. Narcotics officials believe the Colombian cartels, having saturated the US market, are now targeting Europe.

opportunity to open a new market and that the European Community lowers its internal trade barriers in 1993, US government sources suspect that Europe may be where the United States was in the early 1980s: on the verge of being deluged with cheap drugs and unprepared to resist the onslaught.

At the same time, many Latin Americans would like to see the European Community play a more active role in setting and implementing international policy against drug trafficking because it would help to defuse the traditional tensions between the US government and its hemispheric counterparts [25].

Meanwhile, in 1991, the three UN organisations responsible for international narcotics policy—the International Narcotics Control Board, the Division of Narcotic Drugs, and the Fund for Drug Abuse Control (UNFDAC)—were merged into a single organisation: the United Nations International Drug Control Programme. Preceded by the drafting of a major legislative update—the United Nations Convention against Illicit Traffic of Narcotic Drugs and Psychotropic Substances, approved in Vienna in December 1988—this reorganisation has created, for the first time, an effective international structure for implementing narcotics policy on a multilateral basis. In other words, the US preoccupation with narcotics law enforcement and control, the rising concern of European governments about drug consumption, and the increased awareness among Third World governments that the narcotics trade could also bear down on them have combined to create an international vehicle for pursuing a multilateral dialogue, potentially "de-Americanising" the narcotics issue, and finding a more feasible balance to international policy components.

Yet, as the conference in Lima showed, the United States and other governments have yet to convince broader segments of Latin American, Asian and European publics that it is worth the sacrifice and investment to rid the source countries of the narcotics trade and reduce their own domestic drug consumption. Governments may enter into bilateral and multilateral agreements for narcotics control, but it remains to be seen if these agreements can be translated into effective measures that win acceptance.

Setting the context

For any policy to be effective in source countries, it is necessary to examine narcotics cropping and trafficking in the national and local contexts of developing societies. The five case studies in this book each highlight a different facet of the narcotics control dilemma in the Third World.

In one corner of the Golden Triangle, Thailand has made an extended effort over the past decade to provide a multi-tier narcotics control policy. Since the 1960s, Thailand has been the national opium-growing area that has been most intensively studied by

Bolivian villagers chewing coca leaves at a wedding. Coca played an important symbolic and religious role in Andean society long before it provided impoverished peasants with their most profitable cash crop.

development experts, anthropologists and other researchers. Their understanding of the underlying historical and cultural issues in Thailand has helped make its development programmes an example for other source countries.

The study of Pakistan in Southwest Asia shows how vulnerable developing countries can be to a domestic drug problem, how such a problem weighs heavily on these countries' scarce resources, and how it is linked with regional issues that stretch across national boundaries—in this case, the Golden Crescent. Events in Iran and Afghanistan have led to an increase in heroin consumption that has overwhelmed public health and education efforts to contain it. Modest efforts at development schemes in Pakistan that seek to replace opium with other crops seem paltry when applied to production in Afghanistan, which has been effectively immune to international narcotics control efforts.

In the Andean region, the connection between narcotics cropping and trafficking is more recent and direct than it is in Asia. In Colombia, a combination of conditions, such as inadequate development policies, institutional weaknesses and a sub-culture of violence, prepared the social terrain for a crop that was neither indigenous to the country's Amazon rainforest nor linked to traditional consumption. In Peru, where cocaine trafficking has created a new kind of urban culture, a gold-rush town, and a war zone, the various ways in which drug trafficking has affected the local economies are evident. In Bolivia, on the other hand, the coca harvest has produced growers' organisations that have pioneered the settlement of the tropical foothills, governed the growing areas by communal spirit, and challenged the national government.

Throughout the world, the narcotics trade has combined and reacted in a complex, unpredictable chemistry, with often isolated rural populations, with the troubled national settings in which they live, and with the bottlenecks of Third World development. Few, even those who claim to have an answer to the narcotics puzzle, have come to understand the full consequences of narcotics cropping and trafficking or the countermeasures intended to control the trade. What is needed is a willingness to listen to those who have witnessed this situation develop—before any attempts are made to lay down the law.

THAILAND

New Angles in the Golden Triangle

In the discouraging history of the Asian heroin trade, Thailand alone has succeeded in making modest inroads into reducing opium production. Current output, which has not surpassed 50 tonnes in more than a decade, amounts to roughly a quarter of what Thailand produced in the mid-1960s. Opium production dropped from 175 tonnes in 1971 to 30 tonnes in 1989. Sadly, much of this decline has been a positive by-product of an overall negative trend: over the past five decades, the natural habitat of hilltop forest cover, where the hill tribes engage in the slash-and-burn agriculture associated with opium cultivation, has been shrinking at an increasing rate. Moreover, population pressure on the land and a massive lumber industry are steadily destroying virgin forests [1].

Yet there is also genuine credit due for the drop in opium production, as the Thai government and the international community have worked to provide development options for the hill tribe opium growers. Five international programmes, all started in the late 1970s or early 1980s, have worked directly with the Thai government on the northern frontier in Thailand's slice of the Golden Triangle: the United Nations Highland Agricultural Marketing and Production Project; the Australia Highland Agricultural and Social Development Project; the German Highland Development Programme; the Norwegian Church Aid Highland Development Project; and the Mae Chaem Highland Watershed Development Project, sponsored by the US Agency for International Development (USAID). Despite differing methods and resources, all five have helped reduce the hill tribes' dependence on opium crops. A sixth development programme, the Royal Northern Project sponsored by Thailand's King Bhumibol Adulyadej, has also played a role in opium control and alternative farming.

In a study [2] on Thailand by the United Nations Fund for Drug Abuse Control (UNFDAC), the authors singled out the seven factors that account for the six programmes' success:

- The carrot-and-stick combination of development schemes and law enforcement was used judiciously. In some cases, communities were given four years' notice to give up their poppy fields before eradication crews and police moved in.

- Road construction and education services helped hill tribes integrate themselves into the national market and society.

- Thailand's growing economic prosperity opened up other opportunities for employment elsewhere in the country, so developers did not have to provide options that would absorb the whole labour force involved in opium cultivation.

- Improved cropping systems and new seed varieties were attractive to farmers. Research is an important component in developing appropriate technologies, which must be adaptable to varied ecological conditions.

- No unified opposition to opium suppression, either militarily or politically, emerged among or around the separate hill tribes in northern Thailand.

- The Thai government and international development agencies maintained high per capita investment for the target population over an extended period.

- The king provided political leadership and support for the development initiative. This assistance was necessary because the ethnic factor might otherwise have pushed the Thai government toward a more repressive approach.

Thailand's strong track record stems from the accumulated work of these six different programmes. Thai journalist **Charunee Normita Thongtham**, who writes for the *Bangkok Post*, visited the Royal Northern Project in Chiang Mai, 600 km (373 miles) northwest of Bangkok, to get a first-hand look at how one of these development programmes works. Although the Royal Northern Project may have its flaws—being overly paternalistic and scattering its development efforts over a broad area, for example—it does illustrate why Thailand alone among source countries has made headway against opium cropping.

Fruitful harvest from alternative crops
by Charunee Normita Thongtham

At Mon Ya village, near the town of Chiang Mai in northwestern Thailand, Ning Sae Lae confesses to having planted opium poppies. He is a member of the Hmong hill tribe, one of the Thai ethnic minorities most involved in poppy growing.

"Mon Ya used to be among the top 10 producers of opium poppies in Chiang Mai, but not any more," says Ning, who used to be the village chief. "Fruit is better, not only because it earns more money, but also because there's no need to fear anything when selling it. With opium, we lived in fear that we would get caught."

The fruit trees-for-opium venture is one of the initiatives of the Royal Northern Project, which operates under the auspices of King Bhumibol Adulyadej, Thailand's constitutional monarch and an advocate for the hill tribes. One of six development programmes in Thailand aimed at weaning the hill tribes away from the opium poppy, the project has laboured longer than any other organisation to make progress in the Golden Triangle.

Pointing at Chanruk Pimsaree, a project extension worker, Ning says, "I started planting pear trees nine years ago, when he came with saplings and told me to plant them. Since then I have planted more than 30 rai [5 hectares] with pears and another 5 rai with apples. The trees started to bear fruit four years after planting. Now I earn an average of 20,000 baht (US$800) per rai from the trees already bearing fruit." Now the proud owner of a Toyota pickup truck, Ning adds, "The most I could make from opium was 10,000 baht per rai, and that's when the weather was favourable and the yield exceptionally good."

Although the Thai government banned the cultivation of opium poppies in 1959, the ban had little impact on the trade. This was because the government had only marginal control over the northern region and proved no match against the large, well-armed narcotrafficking operations. The merchants who processed the opium into heroin and the drug dealers who marketed the finished products continued to earn millions from their activities. The hill tribes who planted the opium poppies, however, lived in poverty.

There were no research and development programmes to help provide the hill tribes with alternative crops or income. Growers depended on ash from burned vegetation to supplement soil nutrients. When the land became infertile, usually after four or five years of continuous cultivation, the hill tribes moved to another location and cleared a new piece of land in the forest.

The plight of the hill tribes drew the attention of King Bhumibol. Like the Thai government, he was concerned on two accounts: he feared that the hill tribes posed a threat to national security because Thais saw them as outsiders, and he knew that their slash-and-burn method of agriculture (*swidden*) endangered the country's watershed management. He also wanted to reduce opium consumption among them. But rather than attacking the hill tribes as outsiders, he set up the Royal Northern Project in 1969 to provide direct assistance.

The project's goal was not to force the hill tribes to plant legal crops, but to show them that there were alternatives to the opium poppy. The project managers thought the tribespeople could earn a livelihood, and probably even more, from fruit trees, vegetables and flowers rather than from poppies.

"The Royal Project has nothing to do with opium repression," explains Suthat Pleumpanya, office manager of the project in Chiang Mai. "Our duty is development, but we don't keep the police from carrying out their duties. We made it clear to [the tribespeople] that they might get caught if they planted opium poppies. We did ask the police to be lax and give the hill tribes time to stop opium cultivation. Now that the villagers are better informed and know how to plant other crops, the police have become stricter."

The Royal Project's first research station was in Doi Ang Khang, a mountain village and a major opium production area in Chiang Mai province. During a visit to the hill villagers, the king observed

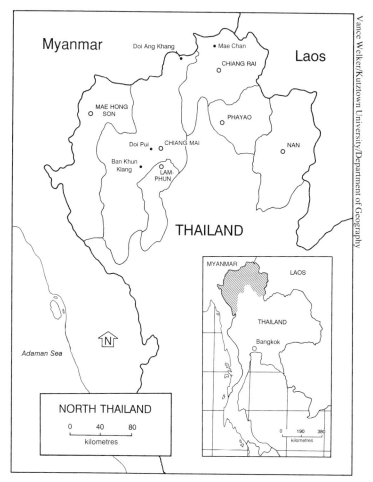

Vance Welker/Kurztown University/Department of Geography

that some of the Hmong and Chinese Haw who had settled down in Doi Ang Khang grew peaches. The trees were genetically exhausted, however, and bore little fruit. The king asked researchers at Kasetsart University's Department of Agriculture to find ways to help the hill tribes. The researchers used some abandoned land as an experimental station and demonstration site for improved varieties of peach and other fruit trees.

"Fruit trees are perennial crops," explained Professor Pavin Punsri, who headed the research team. "The king hoped that if the hill tribes planted trees instead of poppies, they would be encouraged to stay permanently in one place, thus solving the problem of deforestation as well as drug production."

Four years earlier, Professor Pavin had set up the Highland Agriculture Project of Kasetsart to make use of land cultivated and then abandoned by the hill tribes. The project started by planting apple, pear, peach, plum and Japanese apricot trees on Doi Pui, another mountain in Chiang Mai. When the trees obviously thrived in Thailand's highland climate, other fruits such as strawberry, raspberry, blueberry, blackberry and kiwi were tried. The work, however, advanced at a snail's pace.

"We were not familiar with agricultural practices in the highlands, and we had to start from scratch," Professor Pavin said. "We had to analyse soil and be especially careful in using insecticides and fertilisers, as water might carry away residues and affect the people in the lowlands. Also, we had to watch water usage; otherwise, there would be nothing left for the lowlanders to use. And, of course, we had to be careful of soil erosion. It took time before we had the courage to promote agriculture in the mountains."

"But," he added, "our main problem was money. To buy equipment, we had to wait for two years before the government could assign us a budget."

When the king heard of Professor Pavin's project and the problems facing the researchers, he dipped into his own pocket to enable their work to continue, setting up the Royal Northern Project to provide funds and coordinate efforts. As a result of his initiative, several countries offered help through their embassies in Bangkok. The United States gave funding for several agricultural research projects. Japan gave tractors, jeeps and vans for transport. Taiwan, Israel, Britain and several other countries provided seeds, plant stocks and technical help.

Volunteers from the forestry and agriculture departments of Chiang Mai University and from the Applied Scientific Research Corporation joined volunteers from Kasetsart University in doing research and teaching the hill tribes new agricultural techniques. The Departments of Highways, Irrigation, and Land Development helped build roads and irrigation systems and rationalise land use.

At first, the hill tribes were given fruit saplings. Then, so they

Ning Sae Lae (centre) discusses when to harvest his apples with project manager Suthat Pleumpanya (left).

could earn some money while these were growing, they received seeds and fertilisers to cultivate flowers and vegetables between the rows of fruit trees.

Not all the hill tribes readily accepted the new technology. But as they saw that the vegetables and flowers indeed earned money, they eventually followed suit. Some still planted opium poppies, although they did so on the sly; they claimed it was for their own use—as medicine—as well as for elderly tribe members who had developed an opium dependency. After a grace period, during which some hill tribes planted less opium each year while learning to adapt to planting alternative crops, the Police Narcotics Suppression Unit became stricter in eradicating opium production.

Harvesting 20 years of work

It has been two decades since the Royal Project started. Now, depending on the season in Doi Ang Khang, visitors are greeted by the sweet smell of ripening pears or apricots, peaches or plums, persimmons or apples, and varieties of flowers normally seen only in temperate or sub-tropical countries; and the hills are blanketed with patches of green peas, baby carrots, cabbages, broccoli, brussels sprouts, potatoes, tomatoes, lettuce or other vegetables. Forest trees are rehabilitating the slopes destroyed years earlier by the hill tribes' slash-and-burn practice. And with the villagers earning thousands of baht each year selling new crops, the cultivation of opium poppies on the Thai side of the Golden Triangle has dropped.

The Royal Project has not confined itself to Doi Ang Khang. Over the years it has spread to other mountain villages, not only in Chiang Mai but also in the other northern provinces of Chiang Rai, Mae Hong Son and Lamphun. To date, it has six research stations and 21 development centres aiming to help 267 villages with a combined population of 53,400. The government has also put in schools, and roads for market access.

Besides agricultural development, the hill tribes receive assistance for fisheries, animal husbandry, health care and nutrition. The Royal Project also markets the tribes' products. Refrigerated delivery trucks fetch the produce from several mountain stations and bring it to the Chiang Mai University compound, where the crops are packed for distribution to hotels and supermarkets in Chiang Mai and Bangkok or processed into pickles, jams and wines.

During the early stages of the project, the king started a canning factory in Chiang Mai's Fang district to create a market for the agricultural crops as well as to solve the problem of spoilage. Later, when the Royal Project expanded its activities to other provinces, another canning factory was built in the Mae Chan district of Chiang Rai. Now the two factories produce canned tomato paste, bamboo shoots, baby corn, peaches, pears and strawberries. Like the other agricultural crops produced by the hill tribes, the canned products are marketed under the Doi Kham (Golden Mountain) trademark.

"The Royal Project is unique in that it provides everything from irrigation to seeds, fertilisers, pesticides, technical know-how and markets for the farm products," says Prince Bhasadej Rajani, director of the project. "Only the technical know-how is free. If [the tribespeople] do not have the cash, they can pay after the Royal Project has sold their products."

Even though the project deducts 20% from sales to cover its service costs, the hill tribes' collective earnings keep increasing. Monthly income went up from 2.5 million baht (about US$100,000) in 1987 to about 4 million baht (US$160,000) in 1989. The hill tribes themselves say they never earned that much money from opium poppies. Their new-found income is visible in their improved houses and in the pickup trucks and motorcycles parked in front.

Gaining cooperation

One village that has changed during the past four years is Ban Khun Klang in Chiang Mai's Doi Inthanon, where the Royal Project started a research station in 1979. In fact, it has become the showcase of the project's merits, where all visiting journalists are taken. The extension workers introduced sub-tropical flowers, strawberries, pomegranates, apples, kiwi and seedless grapes. Gone now are the shabby shacks this writer saw during a visit in 1986; in their place stand small but well-built houses of wood and corrugated iron. The yards are well swept, and rubbish put away in dustbins. The village has its own temple and school, both neatly made of wood and corrugated iron. At the entrance to the village, an enterprising fisherman has built a shack where his fellow villagers have their pickup trucks or motorcycles filled with petrol from a row of oil drums.

"We all owe this prosperity to the Royal Project," says Krai Sae Wa, the village chief in Ban Khun Klang. "When the [research] station started, villagers showed little interest because they did not understand the project's objectives. As the years passed, we gradually gave our cooperation by planting the crops it introduced."

"Each square metre of chrysanthemums earns a profit of 200 baht [about US$8], compared with 3-4 baht for opium poppies," says William Bourne, a British post-harvest expert sent by the United Nations Development Programme (UNDP) to organise training activities for field extension staff. The UNDP gave the Royal Project US$361,600 to install cold storage facilities at four major

A Hmong woman waters her chrysanthemum plants in the community greenhouse.

stations and to purchase refrigerated trucks.

"After all the expenses for seeds, fertilisers, pesticides and plastic covers have been deducted, villagers still earn 50 times more money from each square metre of cut flowers than from opium," Bourne says. "Therefore, opium poses no problem because farmers would choose to plant flowers."

Although flower growers can plant four to six crops a year, earning an annual profit of 800-1,200 baht (US$32-$48) per square metre, many of the hill tribes prefer to plant fruit and vegetables because of the high capital investment needed for flower production. "There are times when the growers all want to plant the same vegetables," Bourne says. "As a result, there is an oversupply in the market, especially in the cold season when vegetables grow at their best, while in the hot and wet seasons, there is an undersupply of the crops."

"We do have marketing problems," admits Suthat, the project's office manager in Chiang Mai. "The quality of the products is not yet as good as we would like. Because of the distance between farm gate and markets, damage to the crops is high. So we export canned fruit worth millions of baht to Japan. Dried flowers are selling well, from 1.3 million baht to 4.7 million baht [US$52,000-$188,000] last year."

Dried flowers, one of the project's successes, became a viable product when the US Department of Agriculture funded research to find uses for the leaves of ferns growing wild on the mountains. As researchers discovered how to bleach, dry and dye the leaves for decorative use, the hill tribes earned extra income collecting the leaves and selling them to the Royal Project. Later, the project included flowers either collected in the wild or planted, not only by the hill tribes but also by villagers in the impoverished northeastern region. Villagers in other parts of the country have benefited, too, by making the wicker baskets used in flower arrangements.

Vijit Thanormthin, northern agricultural inspector of Thailand's Department of Agriculture, who has been doing volunteer work with the Royal Project for years, sees coffee as another excellent opium substitute. Coffee was first introduced in 1969, but a rust virus discouraged widespread planting. Researchers spent several years finding rust-resistant varieties, which began to be planted widely in 1982. "Coffee arabica can be cultivated at elevations where opium poppies used to be planted," said Vijit. "It is not difficult to grow, maintain or transport. It is not perishable, and it can be stored for a long time."

"Consumer demand for coffee arabica is relatively high," he added. "The government has banned the import of unprocessed coffee, so there is a good chance to develop the local market for hill tribe coffee. The Royal Project has 10 stations doing work on coffee—from research to extension work and marketing—with a total production of 90 tonnes a year. Only 3% of the hill tribes' overall earnings comes from coffee, but I believe it will someday become one of the main money-makers for tribal villagers."

Getting the hill tribes to plant coffee was not easy, Vijit recalls. "To solve the problem, we set up a demonstration plot, with one village selected as a model for the rest. Three or four years after planting, villagers earned between 12,000 and 14,000 baht (US$460 and US$560) per rai (one-sixth of a hectare) from coffee. Last year, tribesmen in a village in Doi Saket collectively earned more than 1 million baht from coffee alone, so now even hill tribes outside the Royal Project areas are beginning to plant coffee."

Crop substitution is not without problems. Some crops require increased tree clearing, and greater use of pesticides, which can mean reduced and polluted water supplies for lowland farmers.

No simple answers

The Royal Project's success with the hill tribes and the resultant improvements to their lives have not been entirely welcomed by other groups. Lowland villagers claim that the opium substitution projects have led to more forests being destroyed for the cultivation of fruit and vegetables, and to water becoming polluted from use of pesticides in the highlands.

Suthat denied this. "One of our objectives", he says, "is to stop deforestation. We emphasise intensive agriculture, in which villagers plant crops on the same piece of land two or three times a year. There's no need for the hill tribes to clear more forest because the crops they plant are labour-intensive. The most each family can manage is half an acre of strawberries, for example." According to Dr Nuchnart Jonglaekha, head of the project's Highland Plant Protection Programme, "In planting crops, farmers need to use chemicals, but we make sure that the pesticides they use do not leave heavy residues in the soil." That, she adds, is why the project provides the fertilisers and pesticides used by the hill tribes: so that extension workers can control their use. However, most villagers who have adopted substitute crops still practice *swidden* agriculture.

PAKISTAN

National Upheavals, Regional Repercussions

Like the French Connection and the Golden Triangle, the Golden Crescent was a journalistic creation—a catchy phrase to group three countries, each producing and consuming opium. This kind of metaphor endures, however, because there is a basis of truth to its generalities.

The hill tribes of Afghanistan and Pakistan were initially part of a supply network organised to satisfy the demands of an estimated 2 million opium users in Iran, and only marginally linked with world demand for narcotics. Then came the Iranian revolution in 1979, the first event to give more substance to the image of the Golden Crescent. The Islamic fundamentalist uprising sent a wave of immigrants into Pakistan, fleeing the social and political upheaval. It also disrupted traditional supply networks, so that opium harvests piled up in the growing regions of Pakistan and Afghanistan and drove Golden Crescent drug traffickers to seek new markets, including some in Europe and the United States.

That same year, the Soviets intervened in Afghanistan to prop up a puppet regime in the capital city of Kabul. To escape the fighting, 3 million Afghans sought refuge in Pakistan and another million fled to Iran. The Afghan *mujahedin* resistance movement, already sharply divided along tribal and religious lines, found itself splintered over the issue of narcotics production and trafficking. Some guerrilla factions opposed these activities on religious grounds; a second group pragmatically accepted them as a survival tactic for peasants or an expedient means of financing their fighting units; and a third sector engaged in refining and trafficking for sheer profit.

Even the Soviet withdrawal from war-torn Afghanistan in late 1989 did not bring a respite from strife. The Kabul regime held on to the major cities, and the guerrillas continued their infighting. Because the war had ravaged the agricultural infrastructure—for example, the irrigation systems—as well as market outlets for other kinds of produce, refugees returning to their homeland turned to opium as a quick cash crop. And because the stalemate between government and guerrillas precluded any effective management of Afghanistan's growing areas, the country was immune to international efforts to control narcotics.

During the 1980s, the superpowers trod on this shaky ground of shifting political and ideological alliances, adding impetus to the trafficking. Just as the CIA's involvement with opium-growing hill tribes and trafficking generals in Laos 15 years earlier had played a role in escalating the Golden Triangle's share of the heroin trade, the US government's funding and guidance of the Afghan resistance movement at this time made the US government shut its eyes to the participation of some guerrilla bands in the heroin trade [1].

Meanwhile, traffickers found an expanded market for their wares. Opium consumption, which tends to be confined to rural areas, is often associated with religious or health practices and has always been accepted among certain age and social groups. But because heroin became cheap and readily available in Pakistani urban centres, its spread took on epidemic proportions. In 1978, heroin users in Pakistan numbered a few thousand. Twelve years later, they surpassed a million [2]. The Pakistani government has proved ill prepared to stop the tide.

Pakistan is not alone in Asia with its drug consumption problem. Other Asian countries, such as Myanmar, Sri Lanka and Malaysia, have similar problems. Urban Chinese minorities, dispersed throughout Asia, have traditionally been prone to both opium and heroin consumption. And Thailand, too, although it has controlled and reduced its opium production, still has between 300,000 and 500,000 heroin users [3].

Clearly, the problems of drug consumption do not lie solely with the urban centres of the industrialised world. The social and economic costs of drug dependency can be a powerful drain on the scarce resources of developing countries. From the crowded Karachi slums to the refugee camps of Peshawar, Pakistani freelance journalist **Najma Sadeque** traces the vulnerabilities of an impoverished Third World society to drug consumption and the regional repercussions of this problem.

The Golden Crescent

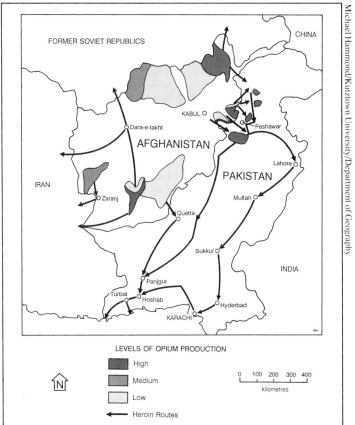

Michael Hammond/Kutztown University/Department of Geography

"God's medicine" bedevilled
by Najma Sadeque

With unsteady hands, the Karachi heroin smoker prepares to "chase the dragon". He carefully rolls a crisp currency note around his precious, dusty hoard. He lights up and statuesquely poses in the "ack-ack" position: with the cigarette tilted upward so that it burns slowly. He proceeds to inhale the smoke, not wasting the tiniest wisp. It is deft work.

Although the denomination of the bill may rise with the economic status of the smoker, an uninitiated observer should not mistake the use of a rupee note as the flaunting of an expensive habit. The fact is that currency paper is ideal for smoking heroin. Otherwise the preferred method is to fill an emptied cigarette shell with a mixture of heroin and tobacco.

This ritual is repeated hundreds of thousands of times a day in Pakistan. Heroin use has swept through the country's cities, towns, and hamlets like a medieval plague. According to figures compiled by the Pakistan Narcotics Control Board (PNCB), in 1978 there were fewer than 5,000 heroin users in the country. At the start of the 1990s, there were more than 1.2 million heroin users out of a total population of 110 million. Another one million people consume other substances, such as opium, marijuana and hashish.

Pakistan's bout with heroin has posed major problems for the country in terms of treatment and prevention, and it has sorely taxed the government's limited capacity to respond to the problem. Although the government and international drug control agencies are attempting to replace opium fields in the mountainous North West Frontier Provinces (NWFP), any success they might have would barely affect the availability of heroin. Pakistan is an opium and heroin importer. Just across the border in Afghanistan,

Opium poppies: the congealed latex is the basis of heroin.

tribespeople are producing 500-800 tonnes of opium a year, although some estimates are as high as 2,400 tonnes [4].

"It's like sweeping the snow off your sidewalk while an avalanche is coming down on top of you," says a drug education adviser working in Pakistan.

Opium in central Asia

"Heroin was really a gift of European nations," says Sajjad Hussain Zahid, director of the PNCB in Peshawar. "The poppy is actually a Mediterranean plant discovered by the Greeks and brought from sea coast areas by the Arabs." At first, only royalty and the rich could afford opium when Arab traders introduced it in the fourteenth century. And over the next two centuries, while the rulers of the Indian subcontinent wavered between outlawing the poppy and creating official monopolies, use of opium spread among the well-to-do. Even Emperor Aurangzeb (1618-1707), an orthodox Muslim and a strict nondrinker, was addicted to the drug.

Further north, opium became deeply rooted in the history of the Central Asian ethnic groups: the Pushtuns, Tajiks, Uzbeks, Qizilbashes and Bukharis in the present-day countries of India, Pakistan, Afghanistan, and what were formerly the Soviet Union's central region: Turkmenistan, Tajikstan, Uzbekistan, Kirgizstan and Kazakhstan. Left with little time for agriculture after warring and feuding, the tribes earned their livelihood from the poppy, which they traded among themselves and with the caravans that crossed the region. It turned out to be their best cash crop.

During this period, use of opium became part of Muslim culture in Central and Southeast Asia on several levels. Even though the Qu'ran gave strict dictates against intoxication, opium, unlike alcohol, did not incur religious disapproval. In the south, dervishes, mystics, "living saints", and their disciples, who haunt shrines and holy places, used opium to heighten their trances of religious ecstasy. (Nor was opium the only stimulant used: for many tribespeople in northern Pakistan, betel leaf is chewed as a mild stimulant, as it is elsewhere in Asia, and hashish or marijuana is smoked with a water pipe.)

Moreover, in the remedies of *Unani Tibb*, an ancient system of healing practised in India, opium is an important ingredient. Opium suppresses coughs and helps dysentery. It also eases joint pains, anxiety, sleeplessness, tremors and other aches and pains. For instance, it provides the only relief for many elderly glaucoma patients suffering from sore and profusely watering eyes. The mountain healers and physicians called opium "God's medicine". For decades, people kept at least half a kilo in their medicine chest.

The plant has other uses as well. *Doda* is a much revered intoxicant that can be mixed with tea to relieve migraine headaches. *Khash khash* is a derivative used for food flavouring. And after the harvest, poppy stalks are dried and used as fuel.

However, when the British turned opium into one of the mainstays of their Asian commercial empire in the mid-1700s, they did not integrate the hill tribes into their production system. The opium grown in the Central Asian region was of poor quality compared with that grown in the fields of Bengal, which stretched for 800 km (500 miles) along India's Ganges Valley. Only when the British faced a shortage because of a increased demand or bad weather did they buy opium from the tribespeople. In the excise books, these purchases were registered simply as Afghan Opium.

In more modern times, opium consumption was legal until 1979, the year in which harvests reached their peak with a record crop of

800 tonnes in Pakistan. Opium was dispensed through a system with licensed vendors, as it had been through most of Asia for several centuries. Some 300 vendors contracted to purchase 100,000 rupees' worth of opium each, for the right to sell 120 kg annually at a maximum of 1 kg at a time. In reality, vendors obtained and sold more: on average, 200 kg each, according to a World Health Organization assessment.

The watershed year

In 1979, this tolerance toward opium consumption changed when the government of General Mohammed Zia ul-Haq issued the Prohibition Order, or the Enforcement of Hadd, bringing the country's laws into strict compliance with Islamic doctrine. This Order included a ban on the growing and consumption of opium and alcohol because of their intoxicating effects. And the ban coincided with other events that would alter Pakistan's drug connection significantly.

"For Pakistan, 1979 was a very bad year," says Dr Malik Shafiq, who has served 15 years on the NWFP National Council for Drug Abuse Control Programme. "Three things happened: the so-called Islamisation, the banning of opium, and the civil war conditions brought about by the revolution in Iran. People fled [into Pakistan] from Iran, the largest opium-consuming country. Eleven per cent of Iran's adults were opium smokers."

At the same time, Pakistan began to be drawn into the international narcotrafficking circuit. Opium was then being exported illegally from tribal areas to Turkey, Italy, Iran and the United States. With the Soviet invasion of Afghanistan in 1979, the last export route was blocked, and opium piled up in the tribal areas. The smugglers took the obvious alternative of joining the streams of refugees and channelling their goods through the hundreds of refugee camps along the borders of Iran, Pakistan and Afghanistan.

As a result, Pakistan was swept by a massive increase in heroin consumption. According to government figures, there were 5,000 heroin users in 1978. By 1983, this number had jumped to 100,000. Five years later, it had surpassed a million and was still on the increase. About another million people consume other drugs, such as hashish and opium. According to a recent study by the UNFDAC

A group of addicts in Pakistan, which has been swept by a massive increase in heroin consumption.

and the PNCB, one household out of nine in Pakistan has a drug user. This epidemic caught the government and health leaders so off-guard that they have yet to make a comprehensive evaluation of the scope of drug dependency and its causes.

Many doctors had thought it was wrong to close down the vendor system. "[The opium dens] were outlets for satisfying the needs of those completely hooked on [the drug]," says Dr Shafiq, who is based in Peshawar. "I warned then that if opium dens were closed to people, heroin would take over."

According to this view, opium consumption did not pose a serious threat. "Previously, we had mainly passive drug abusers who became dependent by taking more than the necessary quantities for medical treatment," says Dr Syed Haroon Ahmed, a psychiatrist at the Jinnah Postgraduate Medical Centre in Karachi. Because opium is used as a self-medication for gastrointestinal illnesses and traumatic injury, users can become addicted if illness or injury requires a long recovery time. But the heroin epidemic constituted something quite different. "Because heroin is virtually pure in Pakistan and not so diluted for street retail," says Dr Haroon, "after a year's use, the local addict is no longer the same person. The psychological and physical damage is total."

Accounting for the heroin phenomenon

Contrary to Dr Shafiq's warning, the opium ban did not result in the old opium consumers switching to heroin. Instead, heroin, usually the "brown sugar" variety, which is less refined than the varieties preferred for export, attracted new users. Its high price gave it an exclusiveness. Some say, therefore, that what preceded the heroin explosion was not the opium ban, but a change in social perceptions among an emerging urban class—combined with a set of events that favoured the availability of heroin in Pakistan.

The heroin epidemic was also seen as an encroachment of Western values. According to Dr Haroon: "[Heroin] came to the middle class and affluent through pop music and the jeans generation—and thereby entered educational institutions." However, this does not explain the widespread consumption of heroin in rural areas, largely untouched by Western customs or urban fashions.

Another theory is that there was a breakdown in traditional values and family structures when Pakistani workers went to the Middle East in the 1980s to work for oil-rich countries and began sending money back to their families. With fathers and other adult males absent, there was inadequate parental control over impressionable sons, who were receiving the kind of money they had never before dreamed of. These consumers were young (15-20 years old), educated and urban. It was common to hear of free heroin samples being distributed on university campuses. Soon after, other sectors of the middle class—the educated, the overworked, the isolated housewife—joined their ranks.

Whatever the cause for the dramatic rise in heroin consumption, the epidemic has so overwhelmed the country that there is no consensus on how to respond to it correctly or on how to provide the resources to combat it. In essence, there has been no serious study of heroin consumption in Pakistan at all, and therefore little has been done to assist in drug rehabilitation or prevention. The public health and drug rehabilitation community, precisely the group that should be leading efforts to apply government policy, has been at odds over the opium ban and the inadequate responses to heroin consumption. And the few measures that have been taken have had inconsistent results.

For instance, to date there are only 30 treatment centres and 260 beds for patients. In Peshawar, where addicts are mostly from rural areas or are children of skilled workers who are away working in cities or in the Middle East, the success rate for treatment has been about 38%. Dr Zaheer Khan of Karachi, where heroin dependency is mostly among the urban middle class and the educated unemployed, reports an even lower success rate of 10%.

Dr Haroon stopped admitting involuntary patients when he discovered patients and visitors selling drugs in the wards. "The whole exercise was self-defeating, just as it is with some hospitals that charge steep fees for detoxification," he says. "It has become a money-making business. Without follow-up and supervision, most patients soon go back to their old ways."

To raise awareness about the repercussions of drug use in Pakistan and break the deadlock of attitude, international anti-narcotics agencies have put increased emphasis on public education and prevention over the past five years. However, until recently, the PNCB had an annual budget of only US$500,000 and practically no institutional capacity to generate programmes.

A Pakistani narcotics official said, "Prohibition creates more unnecessary problems and solves none. Why destabilise a way of life? Why should outsiders dictate our choice of crop just because it bothers them? Can we dictate to them the destruction of their alcoholic drinks industry because it has become a menace for us and the rest of the Third World?"

The frontier provinces and beyond

The government and international agencies have concentrated their opium-control programmes in the small, remote valleys of the NWFP, where 90% of the opium is grown. Population density there is high, and the poppy crop fits into an intensive land-use system with one or two crops a year. The farms use irrigation and natural fertilisers such as cow manure to improve production. Crop yields average 19.9-22.2 kg per hectare, two or three times higher than in the Golden Triangle [5]. About 5,000 hectares of opium are cultivated, though some estimates put the figure closer to 10,000 hectares. This is still well below the peak of 32,600 hectares in 1979, when 800 tonnes of opium were produced. According to some studies, opium represents about 10% of annual farm household income.

Like tribal provinces and agencies, federally administered tribal areas, and provincially administered areas, the NWFP are a loose patchwork of jurisdictions. This jumble of administrative districts dates from colonial times, and the Pakistani government has been hard-pressed to alter the arrangement because these areas have often enjoyed a high degree of administrative autonomy. Each jurisdiction is linked to the national government through special treaties. However, the tribespeople often feel more loyalty toward their ethnic groups on the Afghan side of the frontier than to the Pakistani government. In addition, these tribal enclaves have armed themselves with automatic rifles, mortars and ground-to-air missiles to defend themselves against intrusions. This fierce spirit of ethnic independence among the tribespeople is a major impediment to any crop substitution programme in the zone.

The development projects in the NWFP are the Buner project, supported by UNFDAC; those in the Dir district the Malakand district and the Gadoon-Amazai; and the Special Development Unit, which was set up to coordinate the planning, implementation and monitoring of all the agency-level development programmes. Originally, these control programmes aimed at crop replacement, but increasingly the approach has been broadened to include provision of such infrastructure as roads and agricultural services.

When the US government began to increase pressure on Pakistan for a more sustained eradication effort, the authorities first tried to control poppy growing by building checkposts and sending in the police and militia during the sowing season. Success varied, and then poppy destruction was sped up with aerial spraying from several US-supplied Thrush aircraft flown by Pakistani army pilots. Because the spraying, which used 2,4-D herbicide, also destroyed mustard and wheat, the government had to compensate farmers for their lost crops. These operations have been under way since 1985, but they have failed to stop poppy growing. What they have done is to deepen animosity toward the government and spark off more protest demonstrations. In 1986, the growing tensions over the eradication programme led to bloodshed and the death of 10 people. The Zia government temporarily backed away from its efforts to exert authority in the region.

Under the next government, headed by Benazir Bhutto and the Pakistan People's Party, the NWFP narcotics control programme began setting up industries in undeveloped areas, beginning with the Gadoon Industrial Estate. The government put together a package of unheard-of incentives to attract investors and create employment. Large credit lines with easy terms, electricity at half-price, 10-year tax holidays, duty-free machinery and few limits on imported materials, all of which were bound to hurt already established industries, led to furious protests from investors elsewhere.

The Bhutto government was in a hurry to score points. Businessmen knew the situation would not last long, and the most opportunistic among them were determined to make the most of it. However, this endeavour hardly met its objective of providing the peasants with an alternative livelihood because the industries were not labour-intensive. Nor were workers drawn back from the frontier. Those peasants who did find employment had to be trained to work in an industrial environment, while highly skilled workers were brought in from other cities.

But even successful efforts to eradicate opium production in the NWFP will not eliminate the flow of heroin through Pakistan. Just across the border, Afghanistan production proceeds without interference. International relief agencies and journalists report small-scale production in all 12 of Afghanistan's provinces, the main growing areas being the Nanghar province in the northeast and the Helmand Valley in the southwest. Annual production is estimated at 700-800 tonnes, nearly six times Pakistan's current production and two or three times what Afghanistan was producing before the Soviet intervention [6]. Farmers have little incentive to give up their crop as long as there is no cash alternative in the Afghan economy. USAID and UNFDAC have both tried to set up pilot programmes to work with cooperative tribes, but results are too preliminary and sketchy to say if they will succeed. And most of Afghanistan's opium finds its way into Pakistan, headed mainly for the 100 refining labs on either side of the border—in the Khyber Agency area of the NWFP and in the districts of Ribtatal and Gerdi Jangel in Baluchistan.

Afghan opium grower with the semi-circular knife he uses to scrape off latex. Many Afghans, now returning to villages devastated by years of war, need to earn money from opium in order to rebuild their farms and homes.

Dr Shafiq once took a delegation of US and UN officials to Landikothal and Torkham to inspect conditions in the frontier provinces. They saw how tribal people came and went without being checked by the police. While the group waited at a road crossing, a caravan of a hundred donkeys happened to pass. Out of curiosity, one visitor picked up a cake from a donkey's open load and asked, "What's this?" "Opium," the muleteer responded with a smirk.

With some 200 passes puncturing the Pakistan-Afghanistan border, many known only by traders and nomads, the frontier is almost impossible to police effectively. Pakistani anti-narcotics police have had a chequered record intercepting shipments along the rugged frontier jurisdictions of the NWFP and the province of Baluchistan. In addition, Western correspondents report evidence that élite intelligence units of the Pakistani military became involved in the trafficking because of their role in overseeing the Afghan resistance movement. These correspondents have even reported military escorts for drug shipments, proof that narcotrafficking has powerful support.

COLOMBIA

How the Coca Cartels Took Root

The Colombian Amazon region of San José del Guaviare, 200 km (124 miles) southeast of Bogotá, is not a major coca growing area. Its coca bushes do not compare with the Peruvian and Bolivian varieties in either volume or quality. Nevertheless, Colombian growers planted about 40,000 hectares of coca in 1990.

The Colombian cartels had introduced coca in order to experiment with the production and marketing of a new crop, and created an innovative drug supply system. In this respect, the Guaviare region proved especially attractive. Aside from having the right climatic and soil conditions for the hardy coca bush, the Colombian Amazon region also had endured development models that relied on the irrational exploitation of human and natural resources. This unhappy experience made it fertile ground for the introduction of a new kind of cash crop and made the people particularly receptive to the promise of a quick profit.

On the surface, Colombia is among the most stable regimes in Latin America. A competently run economy and buoyant exports have caused living standards to rise steadily for three decades, making the country the envy of the continent. In addition, a consecutive run of seven freely elected civilian presidents has given Colombia the semblance of institutional stability. Yet beneath this veneer lie deep wounds in the national society. Between 1948 and 1957, a long-standing rivalry between the Liberal and Conservative parties resulted in *La Violencia*, causing more than 250,000 deaths.

Even after a truce, the bloodletting continued as nine insurgent guerrilla groups challenged the Bogotá government for power in the 1970s and early 1980s. These gun-toting political organisations spawned enemies capable of even greater violence. Independent investigators counted 138 paramilitary groups ranging from death squads to self-defence organisations. Enjoying the tolerance of both government and law enforcement agencies, these groups usurped the government's authority and waged war against their political enemies, usually those on the left. During the worst period of

Colombia's "dirty war", violent deaths were occurring at the same rate as they did during *La Violencia*.

The most important phenomenon to emerge from Colombia's turbulent past, however, is the drug cartel: a loose syndicate of criminal entrepreneurs willing to use cash and firepower to achieve their objectives. Although the Medellín and Cali cartels have almost become household names in Colombia and the United States, there are scores of other Colombian syndicates. Most can be traced back to small-time smuggling operations for marijuana, emeralds and cigarettes in the 1970s. The Peruvian journalist Gustavo Gorriti describes the cartels' unique mode of operation:

> Cocaine dealing meant close-knit groups fighting each other for market shares while dodging international law enforcement. Betrayal was common, and was usually dealt with through operational flexibility, good intelligence and ruthless violence. Dealer cartels applied the lessons of *La Violencia*: group allegiance, self-reliance and extensive use of force against all foes. Soon, drug cartels that combined business acumen with feral violence prevailed in Colombia and much of the rest of the Hemisphere [1].

Most of Colombian society has been morally compromised by cocaine trafficking, either by commission or omission. The failure of the Conservative party to take a stand against the cartels paralysed any initiative to turn back these robber-baron capitalists. Only in August 1989, when the Medellín cartel turned its *sicarios* (hired killers) against members of the Liberal leadership who challenged the cartels, was the Colombian government finally driven to action.

Few people are better qualified to tell this story as it bears on the Guaviare region than **Alfredo Molano Bravo**, a Colombian sociologist. He has spent many years investigating the colonisation of the Colombian Amazon, especially the region of Guaviare.

Frontier culture takes to cocaine
by Alfredo Molano Bravo

> Coca came from Calamar. All the good times we've had have come from the south, up the rivers and small waterways. Coca was first brought to Calamar by the Ariza brothers, who had trafficked in emeralds. They were also expert sharpshooters. They landed in Calamar with a small airplane full of coca shoots, took over a large farm, and planted coca. We wondered about all that mystery and just looked on. A few months later, that strange crop was looking mighty nice [2].

Coca did not reach Colombia's Guaviare tropical forest region until the early 1980s. Yet there was an almost fatalistic sense of déjà vu about the new crop and its impact on the region—irrational exploitation of natural and human resources had already scarred the tropical habitat, its residents and their organisations.

Early in the twentieth century, the Arana and the Rosas rubber merchant families, extracting latex in the Amazon Basin, had managed to wipe out the native population. Soon after, the British rubber industries of Southeast Asia took over the market, driving these Colombian entrepreneurs out of business. Thus, until shortly before the Second World War, Guaviare existed only in the obscure chronicles of the sixteenth century Spanish conquest, in erudite geographical treatises and in the memory of the old latex tappers. The rainforest sheltered the few surviving Indians who had escaped from the clutches of the rubber merchants.

The outbreak of the Second World War rescued the region from obscurity. With Malaysian rubber plantations in Japanese control, the Allies discovered the South American rubber trees for themselves. Through the United Rubber Corporation, the United States obtained a licence from the Colombian government to extract rubber in exchange for building a highway from Villavicencio to Calamar (see map on p70).

The US company adopted the same production processes as the earlier rubber merchant families. It hired outside workers to build the warehouses, the airports and the road to Bogotá. Once the basic infrastructure was in place, these contingents of workers became the company's contractors, acting as middlemen in the extraction of rubber.

The company paid for the rubber in cash, which the contractors then used to advance the supplies needed by the rubber tappers to survive in the rainforest. In this way, the tappers became permanently indebted to the contractors. The tappers had to sell all their harvest to the contractors, who weighed the rubber on their scales and set the price themselves. At the same time, the company sold the needed supplies to the contractors at prices determined by the company.

Force of arms sustained this system. The company employees were armed, as were the contractors, and the Colombian government sent an army unit to safeguard the company's property and operations. The death penalty and corporal punishment were common.

At the end of the war, the company simply pulled out—without ever building the road between Calamar and Villavicencio stipulated in the original agreement.

Yet life went on in Guaviare. With conspicuous consumption resuming in the United States and Europe, the contractors and their crews soon found a new economic activity. High transportation costs ruled out attempts to compete in the domestic market. The only outlet was the world market for exotic products such as wild animal skins, and the hides of the jaguar, anaconda, alligator and capybara (the world's largest rodent) fetched high prices. Thus, the former company contractors, rubber tappers, new settlers and merchants began a systematic extermination of thousands upon thousands of jaguars, spectacled caimans and capybaras.

> We would go into the forest for three or four months. The merchants advanced us the salt, ammunition, and a change of clothes. Each of us returned with three to four hundred clean skins, which we had to sell to the merchant who had fitted us out. We received a lot of money, which we would spend in the bars and canteens. Then, penniless, we would return to the rainforest. That was our life [3].

Fleeing *La Violencia*

While the Guaviare region was turning into a vast animal cemetery, the rest of the country was also digging graves—this time for Colombians. The two political parties, the Liberals and the Conservatives, had governed the country continuously since independence in the early nineteenth century. However, with the assassination of the charismatic presidential candidate of the Liberal party, Jorge Eliécer Gaitán, on 9 April, 1948, the simmering rivalry between the parties erupted. The crime sparked off decades of undeclared civil war, leaving 250,000 dead, mostly in rural areas. This period went by the highly appropriate name *La Violencia*.

The Conservatives, who were then in power, organised their peasant following through the police and the army. Liberal leaders organised the peasants loyal to their party into guerrilla resistance forces. The main hub of organised Liberal resistance was the *Llanos*, or the Eastern plains region. Thousands of persecuted peasants fled to the *Llanos* from the Andean regions, where their lands had new owners and their heads carried a price. They fought the armed forces successfully until a military coup by General Gustavo Rojas Pinilla overthrew the Conservative government. Rojas offered guarantees to the Liberals and extended amnesty to those who had taken up arms.

The insurrection waned, but the sizable contingent of men and women who had taken refuge in the *Llanos* settled there. The government promoted the colonisation of Sarare Norte and the area south of the Ariari River, near San Martín (see map on p70). In the latter region, the road built by the rubber company to take latex from the rainforests to Bogotá became the axis of settlement. Gradually, settlers headed south toward the Guaviare River.

From the Sumapaz region, an enormous Andean massif situated southeast of Bogotá (see map), other peasants also came fleeing *La Violencia*. Many of these migrants were tenant farmers who, in the 1930s, had fought for the right to own the land they worked. They had invaded the haciendas and now held legal titles dating from 1936. With the backing of the Conservative government, the landlords had recovered what they had lost, and the farmers were now armed to defend themselves against the Conservative opposition. They became a militarily experienced, Communist-led organisation that refused to surrender arms in 1953 when the new Rojas Pinilla government declared an amnesty.

At the urging of the US State Department, this new government sought to corner, defeat and disarm the belligerent peasants. The army ruthlessly bombed the settlements in the Villarica area. The rebels lost and began a defensive retreat to the foothills of the eastern mountain range. This exodus produced what is known as the "armed colonisation". Upon settling, the rebels cleared the rainforest, planted corn and rice and, though defeated, held on to their arms, their organisations and their political ideals. This core settlement in the Duda and Guayabera valleys eventually absorbed other settlers, mainly those Liberal peasants who had availed themselves of the 1953 amnesty and laid claims along the Ariari and Guaviare rivers.

Extending the frontier

By the early 1960s, the two traditional parties had ended their civil war and set up the National Front. The agreement, signed in 1957, provided for a system of alternating power. The Liberals and Conservatives assigned each other equal representation at all levels of government for 16 years. In reality, the accord guaranteed that no political force other than Liberals and Conservatives would have access to power during the National Front period and thereafter.

The Liberal administration of President Alberto Lleras Camargo began a large programme of peasant colonisation in the Ariari River area. Financed by the Inter-American Development Bank, the programme sought to consolidate the precarious peace and to foster integration of the eastern plains into the national economy. The result was a formidable wave of settlement far outstripping the state's capacity to meet the settlers' needs.

The settlers and their families had nothing but their labour—they lacked technical resources and money. Yet they had to pay for the land the government gave them and, indirectly, for the infrastructure it was building. Credit came late and with excessively high interest rates. Transportation costs were extremely high, since the recently arrived settlers had to occupy areas far from the few roadways.

Nevertheless, the land was bountiful and the peasants reaped bumper harvests. But the cost of credit and the role played by intermediaries stripped the peasants of their small profits. In effect,

Settlers had good harvests initially, but with high interest rates and no access to markets or state services, they reaped no profits. In contrast, narcotics entrepreneurs promised them cash and infrastructure.

the settlers and their families worked for much less than the daily wage of agricultural labourers. Indeed, they might have been better off had they sold their land to *latifundistas* (large landowners) and hired themselves out.

> In a year we cleared five hectares and built a hut. Since the land was virgin, our harvest was healthy and abundant. But what were we to do with so much corn? How could we get it to market? Carrying it out by foot would have taken another year....By river? Where to? So we had to leave it for family consumption, leave it to rot, because we didn't even have any pigs to give it to [4].

Many settlers did indeed opt to sell up; others simply fled from their debts. Most went further into the rainforest, far from the state programmes that had driven them to ruin, and tried to start again, clearing new plots. Within a few years the land they had cleared and made productive fell into *latifundista* hands. Purchase by the landlords was practically tantamount to free acquisition of good land. It also entailed the emergence of wage labourers in need of work—the original colonists, who ended up working on the same haciendas established through the sale of their small parcels of land, as well as the clearing of new areas that would join the *latifundia*

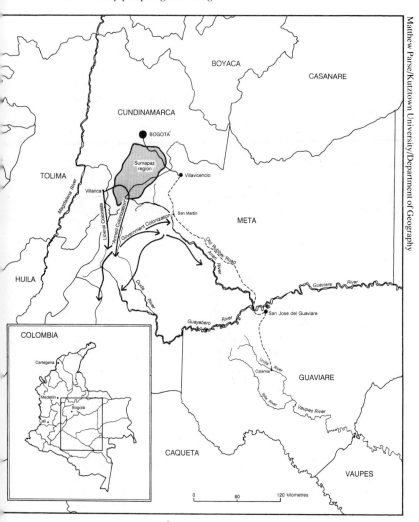

economy later. In short, the state colonisation programme was a failure for the peasants but good business for landowners.

As the colonists fell into ruin in the Ariari River region, they cleared and settled the lands along the Guayabero and Guaviare rivers, following the course of the rivers and the mule path cleared by the rubber company. Within a few years, however, even these immense territories eluded the settlers' dreams.

"Guaviare gold": the marijuana boom

By the late 1960s, history was inexorably repeating itself. Everything the settlers managed to extract from the rainforest—including the land—fell into the hands of merchants and landlords, owing to what seemed to be an unwritten law of economic gravity. Suddenly, in 1975, word travelled from northern Colombia about *hierba* (marijuana), a crop that would grow abundantly if the seeds merely touched the ground. At the instigation of the new trafficking organisations, which would later become cartels, 120,000 hectares of primary forest were cleared in Colombia's Sierra Nevada de Santa Marta in response to the boom market in the United States. The Vietnam war, the peace movement and the counterculture of the late 1960s and early 1970s succeeded in turning Colombian marijuana into a lucrative, albeit non-traditional export.

In the late 1970s, the Colombian government, again under pressure from the United States, razed the crops of the famous "Santa Marta Gold" variety and militarised the northern province of La Guajira. Anticipating the operation in La Guajira, however, the marijuana entrepreneurs had acclimatised the plant to the Guaviare tropical region. The new crop yielded two or three harvests before the authorities arrived and business collapsed.

> The *mafiosos* [gangsters] brought *la marimba*, as we called marijuana. They sold you the seed and taught you to grow the plants. Everyone grew it. I was one of the last. The harvest yielded more than five tons, plus the ounces of resin that stuck to your hands. The buyer gave me 70,000 pesos for the resin and said that he would come for the grass the following Monday. But instead of the buyer, the police came. They stormed in like wild animals, turning everything over....The next day, with my teeth knocked out and having taken quite a beating, I had to go and burn my crop [5].

These two or three harvests in Guaviare—before the price of marijuana fell for good—did not yield large profits for the settlers. But the experience did make them aware of the potential of illegal business and whetted their appetite for cash. The collapse frustrated the peasants' expectations only temporarily.

"White gold": the coca-cocaine boom

In the early 1980s, coca came to the region—like marijuana—by plane, probably flown in from Peru and Bolivia. At first, the drug traffickers wanted to monopolise the operation from beginning to end. They soon understood, however, that profits would be greater if peasants and small farmers grew the crop while they themselves cornered distribution of the shoots and seeds. They also handled the processing of the leaf into cocaine paste and base, from which they refined pure cocaine.

However, preserving all these monopolies in the face of an avid, astute and determined population was impossible. The settlers figured out how to obtain the seeds and the secret of processing. Soon they all became coca growers, processors and merchants, going into competition with the traffickers and wresting some control from them. The farms stopped producing corn, rice and plantain; buyers and traffickers crowded every corner in the towns. The authorities rarely came, and if they did, it was to get their cut of the profits.

Word of the boom spread like wildfire. Thousands of settlers from other areas, unemployed and part-time workers from the cities, professional gamblers, disbanded soldiers and prostitutes poured into Guaviare, the promised land.

> At the outset of the coca boom, the people went wild. They woke up one day knee-deep in money and realized they had been living in stark poverty. It took longer to count the money than to spend it. They forgot about their farms, as if the zenith of the coca boom was going to last forever. There wasn't anything to spend their money on, though nothing was impossible: clothes, gold, food, liquor, women, everything. There was so much money that money lost its value. Along with the cash came another curse, a true curse: life lost its value because one could pay to have another killed, and there was plenty of money around for that [6].

Planes, boats, trucks and buses shipped hundreds of tonnes of coca paste to the cities where the cartels processed it into cocaine. In 1983, the market was saturated, and the price plummeted from one million pesos for a kilo of cocaine paste to a mere 80,000 pesos. The major drug traffickers and traders suspended their purchases. The bottom dropped out of the market completely, and the Guaviare region came to a standstill.

Then came the assassination of Minister of Justice Rodrigo Lara Bonilla on 30 April, 1984. In response, President Belisario Betancur unleashed an offensive against the cartels, in which he brandished his main weapon: an extradition treaty, which Colombia had refused to implement despite pressure from the US government. A few days later—partly because the initial destruction of the distribution system drove prices up again and partly due to production of crack cocaine in the United States—the price of coca rebounded, as if by magic. One kilo of paste once again fetched 800,000 pesos. The Guaviare region heaved a collective sigh of relief and came to life again.

Nonetheless, between the price collapse in early 1983 and the miraculous recovery the following year, things had changed in the Guaviare. The Communist guerrillas of the Revolutionary Armed Forces of Colombia (FARC), who had maintained a presence in the region from the days of the armed colonisation, had won precious time and political opportunity. There were two reasons. First, with collapsing coca prices, feuding broke out over bad debts, unfulfilled pledges and acts of revenge, and the guerrillas were the only organised power capable of imposing order and protecting lives. Second, the leaders of the armed movement clearly saw that a peasant base with illicitly gained wealth was an unconditional ally politically and a generous benefactor economically.

The insurgents had a monopoly on the use of arms—the secret of all power—and institutionalised a system of citizen justice to punish primarily murderers, thieves, informants, users of *basuco* (usually a mixture of coca paste and tobacco) and those who failed to keep their word. The cattle ranchers and landlords had to submit to the guerrillas' prevalence in the area and to pay them taxes. The cartels' hit men and their bands of bodyguards were also forced to accept the guerrillas' terms; they had to guarantee a share of the business to the insurgents through a per kilo tax on all coca paste produced in the area. In exchange, the guerrillas maintained public order, a necessity for smooth business operations. As a complement to this rule, they also mandated that farmers grow 3 hectares of food for each hectare of coca. Experience had taught that, without legal agriculture, the only ones to benefit from the boom were the traders.

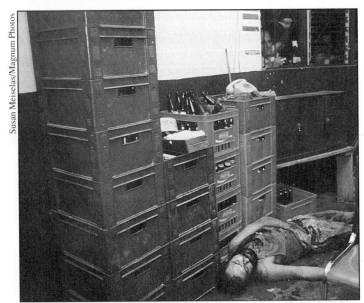

Colombia's drug cartels are efficient and ruthless operators. This revenge killing in a Medellín pool room is just one in a continual cycle of violence.

One day another law began to appear, the law of the *muchachos*, the guerrillas. First they came to say that they had prohibited *basuco* use. They also brought an end to the robberies. Little by little, they imposed order. God only knows what had to be done for the people to get a little respect. Today not even the finest grain is stolen [7].

The guerrillas thus became the undisputed local power in the colonisation and coca-growing zones. The then US ambassador to Colombia, Lewis Tambs, coined the term "narcoguerrilla", which suggests that the insurgents were no different from the drug traffickers and that their main activity was producing, processing and marketing narcotics. For the settlers, however, the guerrillas' role was clear: the insurgents were their protectors.

The "dirty war"

After turning a blind eye to the growth of drug cartels and guerrilla power in settlement areas, the Colombian government in 1986 reluctantly began the formidable task of regaining the lost terrain.

To do so, it had to turn to an army that had proved incapable of defeating the guerrillas for 30 years and that had also maintained sordid ties of collaboration with the drug traffickers. Similarly, the state itself included the civilian government institutions which were not only bribable but also demoralised and dominated by electoral patronage. Through it all, drug money poured into the legal economy.

An unspoken alliance was suggested tacitly by the interests of each sector. The drug cartels were not comfortable with the guerrilla-imposed laws or with the guerrillas' social pre-eminence in the production areas. The army could not advance against the guerrillas, not so much because they were a formidable enemy, but because the law at least formally limited the scope of the army's actions. Local politicians were threatened by the electoral advance of the Patriotic Union (UP), the new political party that emerged from the guerrilla movement during a truce between the FARC and the Betancur administration. Thus, the government opted to ignore the extradition treaty in exchange for the drug traffickers finishing off the guerrillas, including the UP.

This is when the "dirty war" broke out in Guaviare. Pitched against the guerrillas and farmers for control of the country was a frightening array of paramilitary groups financed by the drug traffickers and landowners, armed by the Colombian army, and tolerated by the state. The government's naive assumption was that once the Communists were defeated, the state would be free to take care of the narcocapitalists. Unfortunately, the government and other political elites did not think of reforming the social and economic structures that lay at the root of both the guerrilla movement and the drug trafficking that flourished in the settlement areas.

In Guaviare, the paramilitary hit squads killed many UP activists, beginning with Miguel Rojas, the mayor of San José del Guaviare, and Pedro Nel Jiménez, the senator from the electoral district. Others casualties included settlers, schoolteachers, small merchants, government workers, day labourers and members of the communal action groups. Six to eight corpses were found daily in the municipal dump at San José. People stopped eating fish because so many dead bodies came drifting down the river.

In 1988, Minister of Government Cesar Gaviria Trujillo (later to be Colombia's president) denounced the existence of 50 paramilitary groups in the country. Other independent sources have documented at least twice as many. In mid-1990, Minister of Government Horacio Serpa initiated official action to put an end to paramilitary groups.

The guerrillas withdrew from the zone in 1989 but remained intact. Abandoning the settlers and UP militants to their fate, they simply moved to other production areas where they could carry on as before without exposing their cadres. That was the signal for the army to enter triumphant and reassert its control in the no-man's-land of Guaviare. The Liberal administration of Virgilio Barco, in office since 1986, sped up development programmes, which valiant government officials had been carrying out for years amid the crossfire.

The price of cocaine paste, however, stabilised at 200,000 pesos a kilo (US$400), thanks to the tremendous power the traffickers came to exercise over the market. This sum would not enable the settlers to prosper, but it would not drive them into bankruptcy either. It was enough for them to maintain their status as simple producers.

PERU

Watershed in the Andean Amazon

The boom industry in Peru is no longer booming: for several reasons, the country is in the throes of a major shake-out of the coca leaf market. First, the radical liberal economic reforms of President Alberto Fujimori's government have altered production costs of coca leaf and cocaine paste; no longer are crucial inputs and the imported precursor chemicals absurdly cheap. Second, oversupply (because of too many growers) and disrupted distribution have depressed coca leaf and cocaine paste prices below their production costs. Third, increasing guerrilla activity, more than police interdiction, has augmented the risks. As a result, drug traffickers are being far more selective in their choice of markets and are not buying as much coca from Peru as they did in the past. All these factors auger change for the Peruvian Amazon.

The Andes Mountains divide Peru like an enormous wall. On the western side, the narrow coastal desert holds most of the country's population, its productive activities and its capital, Lima. To the east lies the Amazon River Basin, which contains more than half of the national territory. For centuries, there was little connection between the two sides of the Andes. This division began to change, however, when President Fernando Belaúnde (1963-68) brought the Amazon frontier into the popular imagination by advocating roads penetrating into the Amazon as well as the Marginal Highway, a trunk road that was to connect the whole eastern slope of the Andes. This region was to be the country's breadbasket and provide the safety valve for thousands of jobless settlers.

Yet even with funding from the World Bank, the Inter-American Development Bank, and other development agencies, Belaúnde's dream never became viable. Plans were grossly over-ambitious about what the land could produce and what infrastructure the state could provide. Then, after 1975, as coca became the main crop of the new settlers, especially in the Huallaga Valley, coca-led farming in the tropical foothills repeated and compounded the same errors, drawing in more population than the fragile land could sustain ecologically and economically. In the 1980s, the Amazon frontier region was the fastest-growing area of Peru; today, 250,000 people inhabit the valley. Coca opened up virgin land rather than making more productive use of already settled parts of the Amazon. It continued the exploitation of the flora, fauna, soil and watersheds.

Inevitably, coca colonisation in the Peruvian Amazon collapsed. Among the first to feel the impact have been the townspeople: the middle class, merchants, professionals, and other upwardly mobile groups who profited from the boom along with the coca growers. Another result of this reversal is that it has highlighted the need to rethink the future management of the Amazon environment. Clearly, such thinking should not be limited to how Peru or Bolivia will be able to substitute other crops for coca, but must encompass the wider issue of how this ecosystem and its inhabitants can relate to their national economies and the world as a whole.

What follows is a snapshot of one of those Peruvian Amazon towns that was founded by the pioneer spirit but buffeted by the storms of *coca loca* (coca mania) and violence. Written by **Roger Rumrrill**, a sociologist and journalist who has specialised in Amazon reporting and agricultural development, this story of Aucayacu could be told of many towns dotted all along the eastern foothills of the Andes.

Eduardo Márquez/Panos Pictures

"Coca or death" reads the banner at this growers' demonstration in Peru.

The highs and lows
of a cocaine economy
by Roger Rumrrill

The evening of 18 August, 1989, was a typical evening in Aucayacu in Peru's Upper Huallaga Valley. The suffocating Amazon heat had driven the local people into the town's 50 bars, where they took noisy refuge from the tropical night. The beer flowed like water, especially in the most popular restaurants, El Patio and La Cucaracha Criolla (The Creole Cockroach).

Sometime after 8 o'clock, a few thousand kilometres to the north, a burst of machine-gun fire killed Luis Carlos Galán, the charismatic leader of Colombia's Liberal party and a presidential candidate. Galán's assassination made the government of President Virgilio Barco pull out all the stops in an undeclared war on the Medellín and Cali drug cartels.

The inhabitants of Aucayacu, like those of the nearby coca towns of Tocache, Uchiza, Progreso and Nuevo Paraiso, had no idea that this remote event would have an impact on their lives. Early the next day, the parish priest, some teachers and a few other townspeople heard the morning radio news from Lima and shrugged. "After all, it's only a war in Colombia," they told each other.

Three days after Galán's death, life in Aucayacu took a different turn. The first sign was the deathly silence on the normally crowded, bustling street where traffickers, growers and middlemen traded dollars. The street was nicknamed "Ocoñita" after the downtown Lima sidestreet that had become the dollar vortex of Peru's black market.

Ocoñita in Aucayacu, like Ocoña Street in Lima, is a barometer of economic life. Without Ocoñita pumping dollars into the town's local commerce, everything comes to a standstill.

The coca leaf fuelled an economic boom in the Peruvian Amazon, but brought with it violence, corruption and uncertainty.

Everyone was murmuring the explanation: "In the past 24 hours, not a single plane from Colombia has landed." Ordinarily, five or six aircraft flew in each day. The war in Colombia had reached Peru and Bolivia, the two Andean countries that grow coca, the raw material of cocaine trafficking.

Rubén, an Andean merchant who had settled in the town three years earlier, recalls: "At my market stall, I used to take an average of US$500 a day. After August, sales began to drop and some days I didn't sell anything. November was the worst month. Many of the merchants closed their stores and left."

Just a few weeks earlier, the town's two most bustling restaurants had sold 2,000 cases of beer each night. Now, there were days and nights when they did not sell a single bottle. Cooks threw overflowing pots of food to the pigs. The owners dozed in a stupor induced by heat and inactivity.

The bottom had dropped out of the coca market. The price of 1 kg of coca paste fell from an average of US$2,000 in August 1989 to US$400 a year later, and continued in a downward trend. Worse, there were no dollars to buy existing stocks of coca and paste. After November 1989 and into 1990, coca paste was even sold on credit, a system never previously used for the valley drug trade.

The crisis extended the use of credit to all types of transactions, including payment of school fees. In Tocache, the director of a private school registered the children on credit. The parents told him: "Within a few days the plane should come [from Colombia], and they'll pay me for my *merca* [merchandise] and I will come to pay the tuition."

The coca shake-out affected the entire part of the Amazon region that had come under the sway of the drug economy. Many peasants who had come from nearby valleys—the Central Huallaga and the Upper and Lower Mayo valleys—packed their few belongings and returned to their former homes. They left their coca plots to the voracity of the *malunya*, a moth that feeds on coca leaves. "We're leaving," said one after another. "The coca boom is over."

Sendero Luminoso, or Shining Path, the Maoist guerrilla organisation that exercises political and military control over a large part of the valley, did not look favourably on this exodus.

Aucayacu: coca's El Dorado

Aucayacu is not as old a town as other valley settlements, such as Uchiza and Tocache. During the rubber boom early this century, a contingent of 100 labourers set up camp there to tap latex from the shiringale (*Hevea brasiliensis*), the rich native rubber tree of the region. But in 1914, the rubber fever which had taken hold of the entire Amazon Basin came to an abrupt halt due to competition from the British in Southeast Asia. Few *shiringueros* (rubber tappers) remained after the collapse because the isolation of the area made it hard to live there. They gave Aucayacu back to the rainforest.

Following several failed efforts to revive the Amazon's rubber trade, the outbreak of the Second World War provided a market. Japan shut off the flow of Southeast Asian rubber to the Allied powers, especially the United States and Britain, and forced them to return to the original source. A new "black gold" fever swept through the Peruvian Amazon. In 1945, Victor Langemank, a German engineer, obtained a 4,000-hectare concession, mostly of shiringale. Using labourers from San Martín and Huanuco, he laid the cornerstone for the Aucayacu of today. Eighteen families formally founded the town in 1949. The boundaries were the Aucayacu River and Sangapilla Creek.

The Huallaga Valley

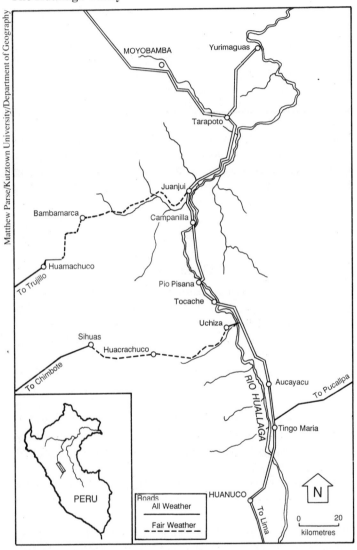

Matthew Parse/Kutztown University/Department of Geography

With the passing of the second rubber boom in the early 1950s, Aucayacu became a centre for the production of manioc, corn, plantain, hogs and poultry. The introduction of outboard motors for navigation along the Upper Huallaga River in 1953 was to have a decisive impact on Amazon life and trade. Now frontier settlers could transport their production to the nearby urban centre, Tingo Maria, by installing "put-puts" on their dugout canoes. And a highway, completed in the late 1950s, linked Lima and the Central Sierra region with Tingo Maria, making even deeper inroads into the Amazon frontier (see map).

The 1960s brought more changes to Aucayacu and other towns of the Upper Huallaga. President Fernando Belaúnde turned the construction of the Marginal Highway into the hallmark of his first administration. This highway was meant to unite the country along the eastern tropical slopes of the Andes, bringing new settlers into the area; construction was started but then money ran out and the road was not completed until 20 years later. A Tingo Maria-Tocache-Campanilla settlement project, funded by the Inter-American Development Bank, raised expectations even higher. New settlements meant the promotion of products such as tobacco, tea, coffee, rice and corn to sustain economic life.

Even natural disasters spurred settlement of the area. An earthquake, which struck the Callejon de Huaylas Valley in the northern Peruvian Andes in May 1970, sparked an exodus of survivors, anxious to rebuild their lives, to the Upper Huallaga.

Yet these expansions never meshed together into a sound development strategy for the Amazon. Although the Tingo Maria-Tocache-Campanilla project attracted settlers, the military government that replaced President Belaúnde had no interest in promoting a frontier settlement, and funding for it soon dried up. When the project ground to a halt in 1975, coca had already been sown in the valley in response to the initial demand for cocaine in the United States in the mid-1970s.

The parish priest of Aucayacu recalls: "A friend from Tingo Maria told me that by 1975 he had 180 hectares of coca. We calculated that, with the sale of one-fourth of a hectare of coca to ENACO [the state coca monopoly], one would no longer have to turn to the bank for a loan. When coca growing was declared illegal, the permits [to grow] were cancelled. Since no one could legally grow and ENACO couldn't buy, everyone began to operate outside the law."

Life in Aucayacu changed, as it did in the other towns of the Upper Huallaga. All at once, the illusions of wealth that had stemmed from rubber or government-sponsored colonisation suddenly gave way to those of "white gold": cocaine.

A "drug culture" spread throughout the Peruvian Amazon region in these years. It was manifested in a colourful, aggressive way as the visible signs of wealth emerged among the townspeople of this new El Dorado.

First were the shiny motorcycles that buzzed along the dirt roads and paths. The Yamahas and Hondas sped down the dusty streets of Aucayacu and the byways of the Marginal Highway. "One way to recognise a common man involved in the drug trade", says a town resident, "is through the first external sign of wealth. The first thing a poor man does is buy himself a powerful motorcycle. It makes him stand out among his neighbours." A young priest from Iquitos notes how the dream of a lifetime for the children from poor neighbourhoods was to ride a powerful motorcycle and spend fistfuls of money.

Motorcycle repair shops began to crop up in the cleared lots on some of the streets, but the mechanics had only a few tools. When their cycles broke down, most owners preferred to abandon them on the roadside; it was easier to buy a new bike than to repair one.

Soon, four-wheel-drive Toyota and Datsun pickup trucks began to circulate on these same streets and highways. The Japanese motorcycle and auto industry found an excellent market in the Upper Huallaga. The car dealerships in Tingo Maria routinely set the annual record for total sales in Peru.

More accustomed to comfort, material goods and spending money, the middle class and bourgeoisie had their own drug culture. They invested their wealth in activities with little return. A quick review of ownership shows that a significant change took place in the property structure of the Amazon, as the drug traffickers bought up everything in order to launder their money. The cocaine boom was like the rubber boom of the early twentieth century in that both were dependent on external demand; both also generated illusions of wealth that ended in dust and ashes.

A bar in every front room

During these years, bars and restaurants mushroomed. In every dwelling, the owner cleared out the living room to set up a bar or a chicken grill. At night, it seemed as if no one slept at home; the bordellos auctioned the services of their women to the highest bidders. The whorehouse managers went as far afield as Lima, Bogotá and Miami in search of fresh talent for their flush clients.

Beer flowed in abundance at night. Any pretext was good enough for a party. There was not a wedding, no matter how humble, at which the host had fewer than 500 cases of beer. Beer consumption also increased when a style of drinking took hold that became a local expression of elegance and good manners: the drinker swallowed a mouthful from a glass and then tossed the rest of the contents onto the dusty ground.

For almost 15 years, from 1975 until August 1989, town residents seemed to be on a steady roll. A few people began to build concrete fortresses, which typically contained the family home, a dry-goods store and a coca-paste processing lab. Most people in Aucayacu, however, preferred to live in shacks or other precarious dwellings. And because most were migrants, they preferred to hide their wealth and take it elsewhere, especially to Lima. They took up second residences, building smart permanent homes in the residential neighbourhoods of Lima, especially in La Molina and Cineguilla, the refuges of Peru's nouveau riche. They educated their children in the most expensive schools. Entire families began to travel abroad; others preferred to limit their tours to Lima, with its oceanfront and luxurious restaurants.

The two main national airlines, Aeroperu and Faucett, made three flights daily to Tingo Maria, with 60 or more passengers a flight. Tickets had to be purchased 15 days in advance. National banks had daily bookings to shuttle the dollars collected at their Huallaga offices back to their Lima vaults.

Townspeople ate well, and beef and chicken consumption increased sharply. Aucayacuans also took care of their health. They built four clinics, one of which rivals the most up-to-date, best-equipped clinics of Lima. The government health clinic, however, was never opened.

Anyone not involved in the cocaine economy could not afford

to live in that dollar-based, inflationary system. As a result, few in Aucayacu—or in the Upper and Central Huallaga valleys and the San Martín region—resisted the temptation of the drug trade.

Shining Path comes to town

The dual lifestyles of Aucayacu's residents—rich in Lima, poor in Aucayacu—began to change in 1984. That year, Shining Path's "urban column" came to Aucayacu and imposed strict and demanding rules on the population. It took issue with the practice of making money in Aucayacu and then taking it out of the region. Nor did it look favourably on prostitution, corruption, drug or alcohol abuse, and the "Sodom and Gomorrah" culture that had taken root in Aucayacu. And it required that each coca producer contribute to the "people's war", either with economic resources or by enlisting in the People's Guerrilla Army.

Anyone who challenged the guerrillas' rules ended up with their throat cut or floating face down in a bend of the Aucayacu River the next morning. People did not cheer these deaths, but they did not cry for them either.

Shining Path's first visit lasted about 18 months. Then the Lima

Tafos/Ayaviri/Dámaso Quispe/Panos Pictures

Shining Path exploited the gap left by the state in the Huallaga Valley, but imposed its rule without mercy.

government handed over control to the army, who came down hard on the guerrillas. The political cadres had to go underground and the guerrilla units left the area. However, in 1987, the guerrillas came back again, this time to stay. Gradually, they made their presence felt, and people began to monitor their own behaviour. This time, though the government sent in the army again, Shining Path held the upper hand.

However, despite Shining Path's stringent tenets, people carried on and made a living. But they had to be more careful and play by a new set of rules.

Coca mania

For the merchants of Aucayacu, the coca economy is crazy and impossible to control. Coca prices have always fluctuated wildly, but they never fell as dramatically as they did after the Galán assassination on 18 August, 1989.

February, March and April 1990 were the critical months for the inhabitants of Aucayacu. Sales fell to almost nothing. The arrival of a Colombian plane would momentarily send the price of coca paste up a few notches, but never enough to approach the old flow of dollars.

In August 1990, the new government of President Alberto Fujimori, less than two weeks after its inauguration, launched the toughest economic adjustment programme in Peru's history, adding to the strain of an already harsh existence. Faced with the previous administration's mismanagement of the economy and an enormous deficit, Fujimori raised prices, creating massive inflation for the first few months. His government also reversed the previous administration's ill-advised efforts to promote agriculture and industry through subsidies for the fertilisers and chemicals necessary for coca growing and processing. As a result, the drugs became far more expensive to produce, and growers and producers could not recover their costs. The Fujimori government's free-enterprise economic policies eventually had as negative an impact on the drug economy as the Bogotá assassination had had the year before.

But the first reaction to the Fujimori shock treatment of price increases was more immediate. Commercial establishments in

Aucayacu shut their doors not only because of the economic measures—they no longer knew what to charge for their goods—but also because of fears of pillaging. In a two-day rampage led by the Shining Path guerrillas, organised bands of looters broke into stores and warehouses and distributed goods among the poor. Several days later, there was a second round of looting secretly organised, rumour had it, by the security forces.

One year after Galán's murder, the price of coca paste fell to its lowest point, US$30 per kg. The producers of Aucayacu were more convinced than they had been at any time since 1975 that the end had come, that coca was no longer the source of their livelihood or held the promise of unchecked wealth. Their distress and disarray was so extreme that they had begun to think—and even to say out loud—that coca and Shining Path were both "good for nothing".

One month later, however, coca paste prices took a sudden leap to US$200 per kg. Colombian planes began to land at the clandestine airstrips again. No one tried to explain the causes of this sudden improvement in the price, not even Rubén, the merchant, who repeated to himself as he headed for Oconita: "The coca economy is truly loca."

Shining Path: Filling the Void

In all rural societies, there is an inherent friction between growers of perishable goods and potential purchasers over the fair price for those goods. Under normal conditions, the state and the market play mediating and moderating roles in this conflict of interests. In the coca-growing areas, however, neither the state nor a truly free market can intervene in the price-setting mechanism in the usual way [1].

Although the coca-growing industry has many of the trappings of a free market (in effect, drugs are sold at whatever prices the market will bear), growers do not have all the benefits of free enterprise—not when their buyers carry around Uzis. It is also a competitive market in which no one knows how high stocks are.

Moreover, the state cannot intervene because it has declared narcotics cropping to be illegal and thus it cannot regulate prices or create reserve funds. It cannot even guarantee compliance with contracts and other obligations, a primary duty of any authority. Nor can peasants appeal for redress, given that they are engaged in an illegal activity. In addition, the corrupting power of narcotrafficking's money can buy off most officials and the police. In the Huallaga Valley, when the law is enforced, it is for profit.

Sendero Luminoso (Shining Path) is a Maoist insurgency that, in 11 years, has taken 25,000 lives in Peru [2]. Over the past six years, in its efforts to overthrow the government, it has made the coca-growing areas of the Huallaga Valley one of its primary theatres of operation. Shining Path is not the first guerrilla group to use the breaches between people and government that narcotrafficking creates in rural societies, but it is one of the most persistent and systematic at exploiting them.

The Peruvian guerrillas are drawn to the Huallaga Valley by the climate of violence that swirls around narcotrafficking. Shining Path has blasted bridges, destroyed vehicles whose drivers refused to pay "war taxes", undermined legitimate businesses, assassinated elected representatives and government authorities, and effectively cut off the Huallaga region from the rest of the country. Only the presence of coca could permit a zone to be cut off and survive. Although Shining Path gives strict orders for its party members to keep away from direct involvement in the drug trade, guerrillas have aided coca's expansion by forcing frontier settlers at gunpoint to add coca to their crops. (Those growers who only have coca fields, however, must diversify their crops.) And throughout, the guerrillas' share in narcotrafficking revenues has been a windfall; their income was equivalent to US$25-$30 million a year when coca prices were at their peak (August 1989), putting it among the best-funded insurgent groups in the world.

Shining Path moved into the valley in 1984 to exploit the conflict of interests between growers and purchasers by applying its armed force to make sure that the growers got higher prices. In the early days, its presence meant that prices paid by traffickers and their middlemen went up by 5-10%. It has also claimed the right to charge taxes for its services. Administering justice with violence, Shining Path represents the installation of a new government authority in its most primitive state. It already considers itself outside "bourgeois law".

Shining Path's network of "people's committees" is in charge of regulations and arbitration. The party also assumes responsibility for cleaning up the area. Prostitutes and drug pushers leave town on threat of death. Young people who have grown dependent on smoking coca paste find themselves forced to go cold-turkey, marching in the bush with a guerrilla column. After the chaos and immorality of the cocaine frenzy, many valley settlers are glad to have any law and order at all.

When coca prices plummeted after mid-1989, Shining Path tried to force prices up. It ordered a boycott unless the few buyers accepted a price that allowed growers to recover their costs. The boycott failed because, despite killing scores of middlemen, Shining Path did not control the whole market, and the valley was flooded with coca leaves. Party documents also show that it tried to open up the market by encouraging Mexicans and Italians to break the Colombians' monopoly.

The void created in rural societies by narcotics cropping and trafficking need not always be filled by guerrilla groups. In Asia, rogue military units, warlords, and ethnic and religious insurgencies fill the gap. In some situations, an entire government can capitulate to narcotrafficking. In any case, the situation in Peru shows how the repercussions of the drug trade, such as guerrilla insurgencies and social violence, feed back into the narcotics trafficking circuit in the Third World and make it more difficult to eliminate quickly.

Shining Path poses a major obstacle to US anti-narcotics policy in the Huallaga Valley. To the already complicated formula of narcotics control, the insurgents add another factor. Not only must the source country and its international allies provide viable programmes for policing, crop eradication and substitution, alternative development, market access, and public awareness, but the government must also take the offensive in a nonconventional war that has already thwarted all predictions about its outcome.

Security in Peru means working with the Peruvian military, which has an atrocious record of human rights abuse, as well as of corruption among the officer corps due to narcotrafficking. For many people concerned about the implications of the US War on Drugs, the prospect of providing military assistance and training in another guerrilla war raises the spectre of Vietnam and the frustrations of Central America, where the US government tolerated miltary and police abuses.

BOLIVIA

Settling Old Scores, Striking New Bargains

As they play delaying tactics to hold on to their way of life, the Bolivian coca growers' organisations have taken the high moral ground in the regional showdown on the cocaine trade. First, these organisations say they are engaging in a centuries-old activity: the native communities of the *Altiplano* have had ancestral rights to tap the resources of the lowland rainforests to supplement the scarce farm and pastureland of the Sierra. Moreover, coca has been an integral part of their spiritual and cultural realm, as well as a commodity. Further, they say, it is not their fault that others —foreigners, outsiders and non-peasants—turn coca into cocaine.

The activities of the growers' associations made it possible to settle Chapare, a tropical region 200 km (124 miles) east of La Paz, by combining the Andean methods of organising, sharing authority and moulding community. It is this Andean heritage that has kept the Chapare region relatively free from the violence associated elsewhere with traffickers, guerrillas and social upheaval. In fact, loss of life in Chapare has generally stemmed from clashes between growers and anti-narcotics police. From the local perspective, narcotics cropping still seems benign.

Coca has become a political rallying cry for a range of campaigns over native rights and broken covenants with the La Paz government. While La Paz wants to hold the growers to the international ban on narcotics, the growers' associations point to past failures of government to provide basic necessities such as education, health and public services, or to respect their acquired rights. And, as noted above, coca is also a nationalistic symbol. Leaders go so far as to say that the US narcotics control policy is aimed at snuffing out Andean culture [1].

It is not clear how long the growers' defence can hold up. Arrayed against them are the Bolivian government, the US government and international organisations—all of which want to ban coca from the Chapare rainforest region. Because the price squeeze is forcing coca growers to start processing their leaves into coca base, thereby adding value to their product to recover their costs, it is becoming harder for grassroots leaders to claim that the peasants' hands are clean. Today, Bolivian traffickers are processing 60% of the country's coca harvest into cocaine [2].

One prerequisite of effective development programmes is that projects go through local governments and institutions. It is almost impossible to undertake viable development work without organising the population; grassroots organisations can contribute valuable practical experience. In Bolivia, both the growers' associations and the central government lay claim to local power. Thus, for narcotics control programmes to be successful there, local organisations have to positively support them, not just accept them at gunpoint. And because these groups are run by consensus, all members have to be convinced that giving up the narcotics crop is worth the effort.

What is at issue in Chapare, and in much of rural Bolivia, is how the new growers' organisations will fashion a fresh pact with the government for sharing both the power and the responsibility for managing resources and public affairs in rural areas.

Amanda Dávila, a journalist working for *Presencia*, a daily newspaper in La Paz, made the trek east from the capital to find out from the coca growers and their organisations what it means to be a peasant in the Chapare region.

Participation, not eradication
by Amanda Dávila

The control post commands a pothole-filled road on the frontier of Bolivia's Chapare region. A police unit in combat fatigues has placed a large sign that reads: "Transporting coca leaf and precursor chemicals is prohibited."

"Identity cards, please," a tall, dark police officer snorts at the passengers in a rickety pickup truck. The passengers, mostly Indian peasants, show their IDs. The police give them a cursory once-over and then wave the driver on.

Access to the area is not always so easy. "Sometimes the Leopards don't just ask to see documents but search the passengers from head to toe," the driver says. The Leopards are the Mobile Patrol Unit for Rural Areas (UMOPAR), the US-funded and trained anti-narcotics police force that wears distinctive drab olive uniforms speckled with yellow. Bolivians dubbed them Leopards, highlighting their predatory reputation.

As the truck finally heads down the road under a burning sun and through the steamy vapours rising from the soil after a month of continuous rain, it crosses an invisible boundary that traverses Bolivia. On one side is the realm of "law and order", and on the other lies the domain of coca. The province of Chapare, together with that of Tiraque and part of Carrasco, forms the Cochabamba tropics, the main coca-producing region of Bolivia. Within the region, countless makeshift laboratories produce cocaine paste and, increasingly, pure cocaine. Hundreds of clandestine airstrips service early-morning flights for smuggling.

The Center for Research and Regional Development (CIDRE), an NGO conducting research and development projects in the area, estimates there are about 200,000 people living in the tropical

Eduardo Márquez/Panos Pictures

UMOPAR control post.

Chapare and Carrasco region. The government built the road linking Cochabamba with Villa Tunari; however, there is no drinking water, electricity or sewerage except in the three towns of Villa Tunari, Shinahota and Chimor. Most settlers grow and sell coca, bananas and some citrus fruits. They also grow rice, manioc (cassava) and corn for family consumption. But coca has been the main source of income for the peasant families since the mid-1970s.

Government presence in the zone has always been minimal.

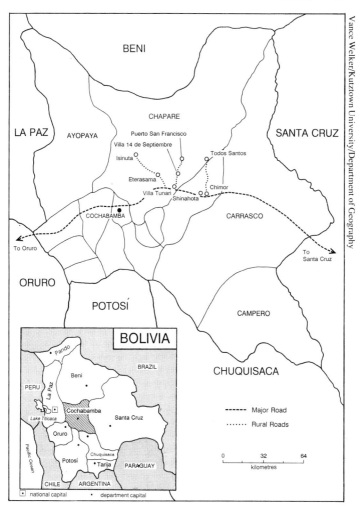

Until the mid-1980s, the state did not bother to interfere with coca production. But longstanding evidence of surplus production feeding the cocaine market, as well as pressure from the US government, led the Bolivian congress to approve the Law on the Regimen of Coca and Controlled Substances in July 1988. It calls for the eradication of 48,000 hectares of coca (95% of which is in Chapare) over 10 years. The 12,000 hectares cultivated in the

Yungas region of La Paz would supply traditional consumption needs (see map on p13). The rationale is that the gradual elimination of coca production from Chapare, or any other area where it was not grown for traditional consumption (coca-leaf chewing), will perforce make coca growing an illegal activity, except where the state permits small amounts to be grown for Indian consumption, as in the Yungas region.

Despite this restriction, coca still reigns supreme in Chapare. According to CIDRE estimates, the area under coca in Chapare in 1970 came to 2,650 hectares, whereas banana plantations occupied 7,000 and rice 2,300 hectares. By 1988, land planted with coca had increased more than 12-fold (to 33,850 hectares), whereas land planted with banana had increased by a factor of only 1.6 (to 11,500 hectares) and with rice by a factor of three (to 7,000 hectares).

Refugees from the Sierra

The first settlers came to the tropical region in the early 1960s, mainly from the high plateau around Lake Titicaca and the upper valleys of Cochabamba. They sought a means of subsistence. Don Pablo Sica, now 58, came three decades ago "because my parcel on the *Altiplano* no longer produced enough to feed my family, and I had to look for other lands".

The National Settlement Institute, a now defunct government scheme trying to promote jungle colonisation, encouraged Don Pablo to migrate to Chapare. It promised a programme of new roads, basic infrastructure, technical assistance for cacao and rubber, agricultural loans and schools. Each settler in Chapare received 20 hectares of land on condition that he or she did not plant coca. However, the Institute never had enough funds to carry out the colonisation programme, and it abandoned the settlers to their fate.

Don Pablo, now living in the community of San Pedro, says, "When I arrived here there was only rainforest, more forest, and bugs. People got fevers that burned them up. Several died."

The threat of tropical disease is still present. Doña Aleja, Don Pablo's wife, says, "We've suffered a lot here. We saw two of our children die: Julián, of diarrhoea, before his first birthday; the second had a cough and died when he was two and a half."

Figures show that the Chapare region has one of the highest

infant mortality and morbidity rates in Bolivia, which already has one of the worst health records in the western hemisphere. These rates reflect a high incidence of gastro-intestinal disease, respiratory infections, anaemia and epidemics of malaria and yellow fever. The conquest of the eastern tropical slopes of the Andes, from Venezuela to Bolivia, has been accomplished at a heavy human cost—because of the vulnerability of upland Indians to tropical illnesses, and the provision of only minimal health services.

The Sicas have four surviving children, aged from 14 to four. All must work on the small family farm, where they grow coca, supplemented by corn and manioc for family consumption.

The family's shack is a two-storey structure built of wood and bamboo over a dirt floor. On the first level, which is shared with the chickens, they cook and store their food provisions. The six family members sleep on the second floor. There are no cots, mattresses, electricity or drinking water. The most valuable possession is a kerosene lamp.

A typical working day begins at five in the morning. Doña Aleja prepares the food, sends the children to school and makes bread in a clay oven. Later, she toasts the corn and husks the rice until Don Pablo and the children return at one o'clock.

Twelve-year-old Margarita attends the school in San Pedro. "In the afternoon we help our parents weed and fumigate the crops that have pests, such as the caterpillars that eat the coca leaves," she says. Margarita's older brother has gone to a neighbour's plot to harvest coca. "Don Angel Mendoza lent us his oldest son for the harvest two months ago, and we have to return the favour," Don Pablo explains. When a peasant has no labourers, he can always count on his neighbours' help at harvest time.

Unions and markets

The Sica family belongs to one of the nine coca- producer *sindicatos* (unions of peasant workers) of San Pedro; the *sindicatos*, in turn, belong to a *central*, and the *centrales* to a federation. The *sindicatos* are *de facto* forms of government in regions where the state is practically absent. They provide most public works and services such as roads, health posts and schools. At least once a week, the Sica family joins with the other union members (there are 180 altogether in their *sindicato*) to work on community tasks. They repair roads, remodel the school and maintain the soccer field. The *sindicatos* also distribute land, organise the population, and regulate the economic and social life of the area. Each one has a small health post and social centre where community members gather to watch television and videotapes.

The coca producers pay the *central* between 1 and 5 bolivianos (US 33 cents-$1.70) in taxes, depending on the current market price, for each 50 lb (23 kg) bale of coca leaf. With these dues and coca tax revenues, the *central* built and now runs the local market.

"Peasants never used to handle money," says David Herrada, head of the Villa 14 de Septiembre market centre and secretary of external affairs of the Federación Especial de Trabajadores Campesinos del Trópico Cochabambino (Special Federation of Peasant Workers of the Cochabamba Tropics, or FETCTC). "Some didn't know what to do with it. At most, a farmer might buy a bus to run a service route, in addition to farming his land."

In 1989, Herrada's community collected some US$50,000 in union dues and taxes on coca sales in the peasant market. With part

Eduardo Márquez/Panos Pictures

*The local **central**, financed by a group of coca producer unions, built the market centre in Villa 14 de Septiembre—government services and infrastructure are virtually non-existent in the region.*

of that money, they remodelled and expanded the hospital, which provides services to all the unions in the area. In 1990 the main task was remodelling the school.

At six in the evening, activity in the Villa 14 de Septiembre coca market reaches a hectic pace, which continues until midnight. Shirtless peasants come and go with loads of coca, dump them on the ground, choose the good leaves and pack them into bales.

Intermediaries visit the market to purchase the raw materials. These intermediaries are known as *sepes* (ants) because they carry the bales of coca leaf on their backs. During the night, these *sepes* meet up with a wholesale buyer who pays cash for the leaves. Many *sepes* are women who approach the producers, bargain for a better price, pay in cash and stack as many bales as possible.

Adrián Pereda is a *sepe* who has been working in coca trading for many years. "Here in the market no one asks where you're from or where you're going," he says. "What is important is that you pay cash and a good price."

The police do not control the sale of coca in the peasant markets. Even so, the UMOPAR forces make surprise raids in the area. "They come in at least twice a month," Don Pablo says. "All they do is leave behind weeping families....They do not respect anything!" During these operations, claim the peasants, the Leopards steal, rape the young women and girls, and commit other abuses against them.

For Don Pablo, the use of the coca leaf in making cocaine is not a problem that the peasants have to sort out. "We grow coca to survive, because it is the most profitable product. It's not our fault that someone else puts it to poor use. We've been lost and forgotten for 20 years. It took a problem that hurts someone else for people to start talking about us."

Sepes and stompers

Those who buy coca in volume pay the *sepes* well, especially the drivers of trucks, buses and other vehicles that take the product along one of the many dirt roads that criss-cross the Chapare region. Some *sepes* work only as guides. Hired to take the coca into the hills under cover of darkness and the thick bush, they ride at night on the coca-laden trucks known as *expresos*. At remote sites, the "big shots" operate cocaine kitchens (drug-processing laboratories).

Eduardo Márquez/Panos Pictures

Sepes *buy bales of coca leaves at the market and take them to the remote cocaine kitchens for processing.*

Feliciano Huerta (not his real name) is a driver who has worked in this business for a year. He notes that, in one night, an *expreso* that moves 15 to 20 loads of coca (one load consisting of 45 kg) can earn 200 bolivianos (nearly US$70). "I made a lot until the police arrested me and I had to pay a $600 fine," he reports.

At first Huerta worked stomping coca. He noticed that most of those engaged in that activity were from Punata, a province of Cochabamba struck by almost permanent drought. They came to Chapare seeking work, first as peons on the family plots and then as *pisacocas* (coca stompers) in the small coca paste kitchens.

In their bare feet, these workers stomp the leaves for hours on end in a container filled with precursor chemicals such as kerosene, potassium carbonate, and sulphuric acid. The agitation helps the leaves release the alkaloids. The stomping process lasts until the mixture turns into a greyish paste.

"We ate little," Huerta recalls. "Maybe it was the vapour from the kerosene and acid—I don't know. But we ate little and quickly lost weight. We had to stomp for hours and hours until the leaves had completely dissolved. Some, to overcome the fatigue, smoked *pitillo* [coca paste mixed with tobacco]. Also, your feet start stinging because the skin burns and strips off until it is raw red."

The stompers' work is hard, and they receive twice the regular daily wage. When the price of the leaf is high, the wage is 10-20 bolivianos a day (US$3.30-$7.00). But when the regular daily wage is as low as it was in mid-1990 (only 5 bolivianos), explains Huerta, *pisacocas* make only US$3.00 a day.

Herrada says that those who work stomping coca and processing it into paste are outsiders who make up part of the "drifting population that is here today and gone tomorrow". Peons, day labourers and *sepes* all belong to this group, seeking to earn a living by linking themselves to the processing of coca into cocaine paste.

According to some estimates, this floating population (50,000-100,000) is mostly composed of young people from the upper valleys in western Chapare, as well as from other departments of the *Altiplano* such as Oruro, Potosí and La Paz. They seek temporary work so they can help their families back home where economic conditions have deteriorated, because of the increased frequency of droughts and frosts in recent years and the consequent depletion of the little good soil that remains.

When the UMOPAR troops carry out operations against the drug traffickers, they grab the coca growers, the small producers of coca paste, and those who transport it by land. However, Bolivian coca growers and their organisations insist on differentiating between themselves and those who purchase the leaf to process it into coca paste. Such a distinction works most as a political ploy, in that it allows them to avoid association with an illegal activity which would jeopardise their negotiating power vis-à-vis the government.

Quick profits

Eterasama, a town near Villa 14 de Septiembre, has become the main centre of sales of basic cocaine paste in the streets and restaurants. "Here, no one can say that they don't have anything to do with the cocaine business," says Cristóbal Peredo. He is a labourer who lost his job in La Paz in 1987 and has since roamed from town to town in Chapare, trying to make enough money to buy a vehicle and work as a taxi driver in Cochabamba.

"Even I have been a contact and delivered drugs to a buyer," he adds. "But I only did it once in my life, and I got cured. The next day, I vomited all day from sheer fright."

"Muelas", Peredo's companion (whose nickname means molar teeth), goes into more detail: "Those who come to buy drugs are generally from eastern Bolivia: from Santa Cruz but also from Beni." The latter region is where most of the laboratories that refine cocaine paste into cocaine hydrochloride are located. He adds that,

Sean Sprague/Panos Pictures

Women buying and selling coca leaves.

as of May 1990, with business bad due to the war against the big drug traffickers in Colombia, one kg of paste sold at a price fluctuating from 500-700 bolivianos (US$160-$230), depending on quality. Once in Santa Cruz or Beni, the price of the paste triples.

Muelas says that UMOPAR forces also profit from the business. Trucks loaded with coca pass through the control posts if they pay 2,000-5,000 bolivianos (US$600-$1,500). The same occurs with paste transported overland or flown out by plane from the clandestine airstrips. Reportedly, in the latter case, the payment may be as high as US$10,000.

The intense trafficking of paste and cocaine has also generated violence in Eterasama. This has helped the UMOPAR forces, supported by US Drug Enforcement Agency (DEA) personnel, to maintain a permanent presence in the area to keep up the pressure on the drug-trafficking groups.

A powerful force

The 40,000 families that inhabit Chapare and the adjacent region of Carrasco belong to 607 producer unions, grouped into 54 *centrales*. These *centrales*, in turn, have affiliated themselves into five federations. This degree of organisation makes the coca growers among the most powerful political forces in the country.

Bolivia has a strong union tradition, especially in the mining sector. With the collapse of tin prices and the expansion of coca growing, the coca growers have come to be the strongest advocates of the trade union struggle to defend their interests against the government and international pressure.

In mid-1988, with the new law against coca growing, the conflict between coca producers and the state became serious. As international pressure mounted to eradicate coca production in Chapare, and the military presence in the area increased, the peasant coca growers began a drive to uphold their economic rights against the government.

The strong sense of community and political organisation among the coca producers has enabled them to mobilise on a massive scale. Hundreds of peasant unions and peasant families have blockaded roads, held marches and staged strikes. Their leaders have organised hunger strikes and peaceful sit-ins at the government offices charged with implementing official coca policy. On several occasions, their campaigns have attracted the active support of workers' unions.

Their efforts have centred on two fronts. First, the coca growers have tried to keep their main economic activity from being banned as an illegal practice and therefore subject to persecution by the authorities. Second, they have focused on making the government recognise their right to participate in the design and decision-making process of the Plan for Comprehensive Development and Substitution (PIDYS); that is, they demand to have a say on how the resources earmarked for the region's alternative development are to be invested and administered.

Their actions have borne fruit. In 1990, the government guaranteed peasant participation in the PIDYS through the National Commission for Alternative Development. However, the peasant federations have only five representatives against the six from various government ministries.

Despite these gains, alternative development has made slow progress. External financing is strictly conditional on government compliance with eradication goals and macro-economic structural adjustment policies. Moreover, the increasing militarisation of Chapare (which includes not only DEA personnel but also members of the US armed forces) has made coca producers more sceptical of the government's commitment to the "coca for development" swap.

Watching the growing military presence in Chapare, Evo Morales, secretary general of the FETCTC, states: "There is a sense of war, a hidden war pursued by the government against the coca producers. We see [this aggression] as a systematic effort to prevent the region's development through psychological pressure and hostile actions aimed at wearing down the peasants and forcing them to migrate elsewhere."

In any case, the confrontation is bound to last because producers like Don Pablo Sica and many others insist that coca is an integral part of their existence and that they are willing to give their lives for it, if needed. As Don Pablo summed it up: "Coca is like our child. It keeps us alive; it helps us send our youngsters to school. Though its price goes up and down, it's still a sure income."

Institutional Options
by Michael L. Smith

The development issues revolving around narcotics cropping and trafficking pose major questions about development strategies, economic policy, institution building, politics and social justice. It may be difficult to arrive at broadly accepted answers in the short term, especially when these answers are applied to concrete cases in individual countries. Indeed, the debate can be highly contentious. Still, raising such questions provides an opening for dialogue internationally, regionally and within each source country.

Narcotics is not primarily an issue of law enforcement but a systemic problem that reaches across national boundaries; the solutions do not lie just in the source countries. Since the mid-1970s, there has been a growing awareness in the North that approaches based on law enforcement and focused on the supply side of the problem are inadequate. Increasingly, analysis of the demand aspect has entered into policy discussions and programmes. In this respect, the North is paying more attention than previously to drug use prevention and public education, as well as to rehabilitation for drug users. In the United States this shift in public awareness has resulted, since 1985, in a reduction by 50% of people using cocaine. However, this change has taken place only among the middle class, leaving a hard core of users concentrated among urban blacks and Latinos, especially the young and unemployed. Most of this work is being done by underfunded state and local governments, as well as by voluntary organisations.

For the Third World, the narcotics issue is linked to the broader question of development and its political implications. For many grassroots organisations, non-government organisations (NGOs), and other institutions in developing countries and in the North, the real question is: What kind of development?

This more comprehensive approach is only a recent by-product of narcotics control concerns, which in fact date back to the 1970s. Since 1972, the development component of narcotics control policy has shifted from crop substitution (eradicating the narcotics crop and replacing it with a legal one) to integrated rural development programmes that try to address a wider range of problems. For instance, the programmes in Thailand provide a menu of alternative crops, income-generating activities, and public infrastructure and services, and they even get involved in the packaging and marketing of goods [1].

But these initiatives have limited resources. For instance, between 1971 and 1985, resources in the United Nations Funding for Drug Abuse Control (UNFDAC) did not exceed US$150 million [2]. Even in 1991, the new International Drug Control Programme had a budget of only US$90 million. In addition, the impact of some of these development programmes has been extremely limited, because they have targeted grower populations in only the most accessible areas. Others, such as those in Peru and Myanmar, have simply not been able to reach growers effectively because of rebel insurgencies. Because they amount to patchwork responses to the need for a development component, these programmes have rarely been integrated into each country's overall development strategy, assuming there is one.

Thus, at best these programmes can be considered pilot projects in designing and implementing strategies for narcotics control in growing regions. Indeed, much research on the narcotics-growing matrix and possible solutions still needs to be done; for instance, the development of new seed varieties adapted to the climatic conditions of a growing region takes years to yield results.

Although narcotics control programmes sometimes call their development component "alternative development", this label has generally meant "alternative to narcotics cropping", as in crop replacement. The wider acceptance of the term in the broader international development community, however, points to a different direction: towards development that is sustainable ecologically, economically and politically, without limiting the prospects for future generations. Increasingly, it is being called "sustainable development".

Sustainable development and narcotics

Gro Harlem Brundtland, chairperson of the World Commission on Environment and Development, wrote in 1987: "We define sustainable development as paths of progress which meet the needs and aspirations of the present generation without compromising the ability of future generations to meet their needs [3]."

This concept of sustainable development takes a long-term perspective in order that future generations are not penalised for current consumption and depletion of natural resources. It also does not overestimate the human capacity to understand and control the natural environment, emphasising instead the dependence of humans beings on their habitat. It aims to connect the issues of poverty and development, and to ensure the equitable distribution of wealth and resources among all people. Finally, it requires that the knowledge and abilities of indigenous populations must be applied to their problems and that their need to control their present and future must be represented and respected.

Sustainable development means enabling marginalised populations to move into the future while integrating themselves into their national societies, thereby encouraging political democratisation and pluralism. It means using methods of conflict resolution other than military force or violence. It means setting up economic systems that are ecologically sound and yet still provide for adequate living standards, thus redressing the unbalanced distribution of wealth and resources in the world. And it means building public institutions into the heart of developing nations—precisely where central governments have failed to engage themselves.

Within the context of sustainable development as it relates to the narcotics trade, there are no easy prescriptions, magic formulas or quick fixes. No viable option will be achieved fast. But the narcotics cropping and trafficking issue unlocks an opportunity that is mutually beneficial to consumer and source countries alike: that of engaging in a dialogue about the problem and broadening it out to encompass the central issues of sustainable development. Thus, the issue is not technical (finding the right crop to substitute for the opium poppy or the coca plant) or legal (enforcing international law) but political: how to tackle the basic questions of sustainable development in the Third World.

From this perspective, there are five spheres in which efforts may be concentrated: international coordination and multilateral programmes; national governments; local governments; grassroots organisations; and NGOs.

The international forum

The international effort to control narcotics cropping and trafficking has only begun to take on momentum over the past 10 years. This is because the US government pushed law enforcement and supply-side initiatives so strongly in the past that it tainted an international approach to the issue. Even where US narcotics control programmes have tried to incorporate a development component, they have been politically handicapped. This is especially so in Latin America, where insurgent groups can target development agencies as instruments of "Yankee imperialism".

As mentioned in "The Gordian Knot", the recognition by the US government that it needs broader world support for an international drug policy, the incorporation of a European policy and the more active participation of Third World countries have created possibilities for a more balanced, truly international policy on narcotics control. The UN organisations responsible were reorganised in 1991 and should provide a more efficient mechanism for this effort.

Regional initiatives also provide a clear alternative to a US-dominated agenda and a way to address the cross-regional impact of narcotrafficking with a more even hand. Although the Andean initiative, which began in early 1990 with the United States, Colombia, Peru and Bolivia, has failed to fulfil all its original objectives of integrating regional initiatives, it has set a precedent. In early 1992, this coordinating effort will broaden its membership by incorporating Mexico, Ecuador and Venezuela. In addition, the Organization of American States has also played an active, albeit low-profile role in opening a regional approach to narcotics control.

Regional coordination in Southeast and Southwest Asia will require more time to develop. Much will depend on Afghanistan and Myanmar ending their internal conflicts and setting up more broadly accepted governments.

The World Bank and regional development banks will have to take narcotics cropping and narcotrafficking into account when planning development projects with source countries, because of the repercussions of the narcotics trade on national economies. But there also has to be a broader discussion about the overall development goals that these institutions are pursuing, that takes into account the premises of sustainable development.

National government

National government should be the forum in which national societies reach lasting consensus on their development goals and establish the institutional means to attain them. Only then can any meaningful attempt be made towards controlling the narcotics trade. Often, however, other issues such as institution building and economic policy will have to precede any attempt to deal with narcotrafficking or related issues.

Local communities and growers, whether involved in narcotics crops or not, base their survival strategies on their perceptions of how their governments will conduct economic policy. Thus, source-country governments must maintain long-term, sustainable macro-economic policies that encourage productive economic activity. Crucial here is an agricultural policy that does not favour cheap food import schemes or make the farmer subsidise the urban consumer through price controls.

Governments and interest groups in source countries have had difficulty formulating viable programmes and policies which broaden the narrow focus of narcotics control schemes and link them to development goals. The slow start of the Andean regional initiative since 1990 has been partly due to the incapacity of the national governments to draft programmes and projects quickly and efficiently so that funders can respond to them. On the other hand, the US government has been slow to act on those initiatives which have reached its desks.

Some governments have fallen into the trap of proposing overblown development schemes, thinking that the huge sums of money moved by traffickers justify investments of the same size by the US government and other funders. Given the hesitance of major funders such as the United States, however, a more gradual approach is advisable so that national governments can demonstrate their capacity to execute and achieve realistic goals. Only by creating a stronger negotiating position and working with other regional governments can source countries improve their leverage and bargaining power vis-à-vis the United States.

Another area that needs to be strengthened is law enforcement and the judicial systems, not only in order to prosecute narcotics cases but also to ensure that the law is applied fairly and consistently in all kinds of cases.

Local government

International narcotics control policy has concentrated primarily on multilateral coordination and government-to-government agreements. The weak link in this approach, however, has been the translation of policy into action with local governments, whether they be municipal or provincial. Although national governments may be willing to implement narcotics control programmes, there are few viable local institutions with enough democratic grassroots participation to carry out such programmes in the field. This vacuum of government was one of the factors that opened up growing areas to narcotrafficking in the first place.

The upshot is that the national government's lack of legitimacy and authority in peripheral regions will continue as long as the local governments are unable to achieve the strength, representativity and longevity required to exert authority while encouraging popular participation in all areas of government. For effective development work, however, local government is the most fruitful level on which to operate because it is here that growers can become participants in, and so committed to, programmes designed to improve their lives, and here that they can see their interests more fully represented in future development schemes.

Grassroots organisations

For any development programme to succeed, local organisations have to support it voluntarily. However, grassroots organisations and rural communities have a holistic approach to their problems in life. Practically speaking, this means that, although they would not be predisposed to join an anti-drug crusade even if it were presented as a product of their own religious or moral principles, they would participate in efforts that promise to improve their quality of living, respect their rights and incorporate their opinions into development programmes.

Peasant farmers and their organisations have a stake in solving the narcotrafficking-development dilemma, as they are often the ones hurt most by ill-conceived programmes and by the consequences of narcotrafficking. Grassroots organisations can contribute their practical experience and knowledge of local conditions. Some coca and poppy growers have already created or are now creating organisations that may become part of the solution.

Furthermore, governments and development agencies cannot expect narcotic growers' associations to make a complete, abrupt break with their illegal crops. Indeed, there will be a testing period in which many growers will hedge their bets. They will continue to grow coca or opium until both national and international partners prove that they are firmly committed to building working relationships and that alternative development programmes will avoid past mistakes, be sustainable over the long term and incorporate the growers' own work. Experience in Asia suggests this process may take anywhere from three years to 15, depending on complex environmental, social, economic and technological factors [4].

The truth is that alternative development proposals may never fully compensate for the economic shift away from narcotic crops if they are measured on a dollar-for-dollar substitution basis. The money moved by international trafficking cartels will always be more attractive than even the most sophisticated schemes to buy up narcotics crops. But this recognition that an anti-narcotics programme cannot outspend drug traffickers does not mean that governments and international organisations should not commit more financial support to both the law enforcement and development components of a reasonable programme. Indeed, such bodies have to put together formulas that incorporate "intangibles" into the eradication goal. Intangibles are those elements that may not have a monetary value but that growers would willingly accept as part of the trade-off in giving up their narcotic crops.

Sean Sprague/Panos Pictures

Unless narcotics programmes actively involve growers and address their long-term development needs, cultivating drugs will continue to be the best means of economic survival for settlers like this Bolivian farmer.

For instance, coca and poppy growers would trade away their "growing rights" for greater participation in local government and decisionmaking over new areas of commerce and production, as well as for recognition of their ethnic and regional rights and diversity. National governments should facilitate such empowerment and demonstrate the desired level of respect through dialogue with the growers and through shared management of development programmes and research. In addition, they should provide adequate levels of public services, such as education and health care for school-age children; doing so gives growers a guarantee that their future is provided for.

It is difficult to put a price on these factors. Indeed, they are part of the pact between government and citizenry. Under the harsh conditions of underdevelopment, however, they are often a rare commodity.

Non-government organisations

Narcotics cropping and trafficking are not issues from which public and private development agencies should shy away. These issues have clear implications for public health and security, as well as the environment and development prospects in scores of countries in Latin America and Asia. Having already proven their worth in specific areas of narcotics control—drug education, prevention and rehabilitation—NGOs are logical partners in a new dialogue between growers, governments and international participants, because they can maintain closer relationships with local communities, assisting them to build on and formalise local experience and needs so they can get across their own agenda to development and government authorities. They can also provide an invaluable service by critiquing narcotics control programmes against the strict yardstick of sustainable development.

Taking back the initiative

Due to the complex set of problems facing some narcotics-producing countries—such as Peru, Myanmar and Afghanistan—it may seem to outside observers that these countries are irrevocably locked into failure. Yet, if there is a solution to the Third World's role in the narcotics cropping and trafficking web, or a way for developing countries to break out of the dead end of poverty, it will come from the creativity and resourcefulness found in these developing nations. Frequently, Western observers fail to see these new initiatives.

A case in point is Colombia. The Colombian government has shown the capacity—sometimes belated—to assume the political risks of cracking down on the narcotics trade. Until 1990, many Colombians thought their society would not survive the capture, trial and imprisonment (or extradition) of a major drug *capo*. The bloodshed and mayhem among rival cartels, the government, the military and the US government would tear the country apart, went the argument. Then, against the advice of the United States, the Gaviria government instituted an amnesty programme in 1990 that allowed traffickers to hand themselves in and face trial for a single offence. Medellín drug king Pablo Escobar and his associates are now in jail awaiting trial, with few prospects of getting out soon—yet Colombia is still on its feet.

Equally striking is the way that, during the 1980s, Colombia managed to coax, harass and entice all but two guerrilla organisations into truces and eventual amnesties that ended three decades of insurgency. The initiative, started during the term of President Belisario Betancur, gained momentum as the narcotics-related violence increased. Today, former guerrillas hold cabinet portfolios and sit in Congress. This reduction in the number of agents of violence within Colombia bodes well for the viability of the society and may put an end to several decades of political turmoil.

Any new responses to the challenges posed by narcotics cropping and trafficking and their related problems must also be matched by a concerted international effort to resolve the underlying links of poverty and underdevelopment. The United States, the European Community and the United Nations will never provide sufficient funding to compensate fully for the income loss or political costs involved in eliminating the narcotics trade. Their resources may serve only as seed money or as proof of a common commitment to the task. Rather than approach the narcotics issue as a problem exclusive to the Third World, it must be linked with the broader question of development. Development alone will not be the solution to the narcotics problem, but it does provide a more adequate platform for dealing with the underlying causes.

Notes

Introduction

1. Smith, M. L., unpublished paper on Narcotics and Development, 1991.
2. Ibid.

The Gordian Knot

1. The most comprehensive study of opium's power in China and Southeast Asia is to be found in McCoy, Alfred, *The Politics of Heroin: CIA Complicity in the Global Drug Trade,* Lawrence Hill Books, Chicago, 1990.
2. Crooker, Richard, "The historical geography of opium production in the Southwest China region", proceedings of the Seventh International Symposium on Asian Studies, reprint, p88.
3. US Department of State, *International Narcotics Control Strategy Report*, Washington, DC, US Government Printing Office, 1990, p22.
4. McCoy, Alfred, "Opium for the natives", *The Politics of Heroin in South-East Asia,* Harper Colophon Books, New York, 1973.
5. McNicoll, André, *Drug Trafficking: A North-South Perspective*, North-South Institute, Ottawa, Canada, 1983, p33.
6. *Seizing Opportunities,* a report of the Inter-American Commission on Drug Policy, Institute of the Americas and Center for Iberian and Latin American Studies, University of California-San Diego, 1991, p15.
7. Farah, Douglas, "Ecuador is drawn deeper into cocaine trade", *The Washington Post*, 4 September, 1990.
8. Robinson, Eugene, "Cocaine operations shift southward", *The Washington Post*, 9 June, 1991.
9. *Seizing Opportunities*, op. cit., p18.
10. Garland, Eduardo Bedoya, "Intensification and degradation in the agricultural systems of the Peruvian upper jungle: the Upper Huallaga case", in Little, Peter D. et al (eds.), *Lands at Risk in the*

Third World: Local-level perspectives, Westview Press, Boulder, Colorado, and London, 1987, pp290-315.

11. Marcelo, Buenaventura, "Víctimas del narcotráfico", *Medio Ambiente,* September 1987, pp8-10. This magazine is the leading environmental periodical in Peru.

12. McNicoll, op. cit., p66.

13. Development Assistance Committee, "Alternative development: a new approach", a preliminary document for the Organization for Economic Co-operation and Development's expert planning meeting, November 1991, Paris, France, pp2-3.

14. Ibid.

15. Kammerer, Cornelia Ann, "Opium and tribal peoples in the Golden Triangle", paper presented at the American Anthropological Association annual meeting, Washington, DC, 17 November, 1989.

16. Development Assistance Committee, op. cit., p3.

17. Personal communication, several economists in Lima, Peru, February 1990. In 1986, Daniel Carbonetto, the chief economic advisor to the García government, said that the government incorporated the availability of narcotrafficking dollars into its policy of holding down exchange rates as an anti-inflation tool and as a means of increasing international reserves.

18. Personal communication, Ibán de Rementería, agronomist, May 1990.

19. Hamilton, John Maxwell, *Entangling Alliances: How the Third World shapes our lives,* Cabin John, MD, Seven Locks Press, Washington, DC, 1990, p11.

20. García-Sayán, Diego, (comp.), *Narcotráfico: Realidades y alternativas,* proceedings of the International Conference on Narcotrafficking: Reality and Alternatives, Lima, Peru, 5-7 February, 1990, Comisión Andina de Juristas, Lima, 1990, pp221-223.

21. McNicoll, op. cit., pp68-69.

22. *Seizing Opportunities,* op. cit., p22.

23. See *Clear and Present Dangers: The US Military and the War on Drugs in the Andes,* Washington Office on Latin America, Washington, DC, 1991.

24. Drozdiak, William, "Europe finds Colombian cartels well ensconced", *The Washington Post,* 11 April, 1991.

25. See Comisión Andina de Juristas, *Narcotráfico: A un año de Cartagena,* declaration of the International Conference, Lima, Peru, 4-5 April, 1991, p13.

Thailand

1. Crooker, Richard, "Forces of change in the Thailand opium zone", *The Geographical Review* 78, No 3, July 1988, pp255-6.
2. Lamar, Robert G. and Renard, Ronald D., "Opium crop substitution without fears or terror—The case of Northern Thailand, 1971-1989", prepared for the 1989 UNFDAC Regional Seminar on Replacement of Opium Poppy Cultivation.

Pakistan

1. Rupert, James and Coll, Steve, "US declines to probe Afghan drug trade", *The Washington Post*, 13 May, 1990.
2. "Narco power: Pakistan's parallel government?", *Newsline*, December 1989, p17.
3. Development Assistance Committee, op. cit., p3.
4. Comment by Dr Chris Conrad, Kabul director of the UN Drug Control Programme, 1992.
5. See also van der Meer, Cornelis L. J., "Problems and progress in crop replacement programme in Burma, Pakistan and Thailand, 1972-1987: a review", pp40-47.
6. According to a December 1991 United Nations report, opium production may have been as high as 2,000 tonnes. This estimate is nearly triple the amount used by US government sources. See "Afghanistan: aiming to be the leading opium producer", *The Geopolitical Drug Dispatch*, No 3, January 1992.

Colombia

1. Gorriti, Gustavo, "Latin America's internal wars", *Journal of Democracy*, No 2, Winter 1991, p91.
2. The quotes in this article come from Alfredo Molano Bravo's personal interviews or from his book, *Siguiendo el Corte,* El Ancora Editores, Bogotá, 1989.
3. Personal interview.
4. Personal interview.
5. Personal interview.
6. From *Siguiendo el Corte*, p278.
7. Ibid., p286.

Shining Path: Filling the Void

1. de Rementería, Ibán, "La sustitución de cultivos como perspectiva", in García-Sayán, (ed.), *Coca, Cocaína y Narcotráfico: Laberinto en los Andes*, Comisión Andina de Juristas, Lima, 1989, pp361-388.

2. Scott Palmer, David, (ed.), *The Shining Path of Peru*, St. Martin Press, New York, 1992.

Bolivia

1. For a more detailed discussion of these political implications, see Kevin Healy, "Political ascent of Bolivia's coca leaf producers", *The Journal of Interamerican Studies and World Affairs*, Spring 1991.
2. Robinson, Eugene, "Cocaine operations shift southward", *The Washington Post*, 9 June, 1991. The 60% figure comes from sources at the US Department of State and has been confirmed by Andean development sources.

Institutional options

1. McNicoll, op. cit., pp74-5.
2. Development Assistance Committee, "The role of development assistance in narcotics reduction in developing countries", a final report from the Organization for Economic Co-operation and Development's meeting of experts, Paris, 1987.
3. Quoted in *Towards Sustainable Development,* The Panos Institute, London, 1987, p*ix*.
4. Personal communication with Richard Crooker and US Department of State officials.

Selected Bibliography

General reading

Labrousse, Alain, *La drogue, l'Argent et les Armes*, Fayard, Paris, 1991.

Lusane, Clarence, *Pipe Dream Blues: Racism and the war on drugs*, South End Press, Boston, 1991.

McNicoll, André, *Drug Trafficking: A North-South Perspective*, The North-South Institute, Ottawa, 1983.

Tullis, LaMond, *Beneficiaries of the Illicit Drug Trade: political consequences and international policy at the intersection of supply and demand*, United Nations Research Institute for Social Development, Geneva, 1991.

United Nations Association of the United States of America, *Breaking the Drug Chain: Options for international policy on narcotics drugs*, New York, 1990.

United States Department of Justice, Drug Enforcement Administration, *From the Source to the Street: current prices for cannabis, cocaine, and heroin*, Special Report, Intelligence Trends, 16, No 2, 1989.

United States Department of State, Bureau of International Narcotics Matters, *International Narcotics Control Strategy Report*, General Printing Office, Washington, DC, 1991.

White House, The, *National Drug Control Strategy*, US Government Printing Office, Washington, DC, 1990.

The Andean region, coca and cocaine

Bagley, Bruce, "Colombia and the war on drugs", *Foreign Affairs*, Vol 67, No 1, Fall 1988, pp70-92.

Bagley, Bruce, "Assessing the Americas' war on drugs: special issue", *Journal of Interamerican Studies and World Affairs 30*,

No 2&3, Summer/Fall 1988. Contains 12 articles on the impact of the drug trade on hemispheric affairs.

Bedoya, Eduardo, "Intensification and degradation in the agricultural systems of the Peruvian upper jungle: the Upper Huallaga case", in Little, Peter D. and Horowitz, Michael M., with Nyerges, A. Endre, (eds.), in *Lands at Risk in the Third World: Local-level perspectives*, Westview Press, Boulder, Colorado, 1987, pp290-315.

Comisión Andina de Juristas, *Narcotráfico: A un año de Cartagena*, declaration of the International Conference, Lima, Peru, 4-5 April, 1991.

Delpirou, Alan and Labrousse, Alain, *El Sendero de la Cocaína*, Editorial Laia, Barcelona, 1986. Also published as *Coca Coke*, Édicions La Découverte, Paris, 1986.

Duzán, María Jimena, "Colombia's bloody war of words", *Journal of Democracy II*, No 1, Winter 1991, pp99-106.

García-Sayán, Diego, (ed.), *Coca, Cocaina y Narcotráfico: Laberinto en los Andes*, Comisión Andina de Juristas, Lima, 1989.

García-Sayán, Diego, (comp.), *Narcotráfico: Realidades y alternativas*, proceedings of the International Conference on Narcotrafficking: Reality and Alternatives, Lima, Peru, 5-7 February, 1990, Comision Andina de Juristas, Lima, 1990.

Gonzales, José, "Perú: Sendero Luminoso en el Valle de la Coca", in García-Sayán, (ed.), op. cit., pp207-222.

Gorriti, Gustavo, "Latin America's internal wars", *Journal of Democracy*, Winter 1991, pp85-98.

Gugliotta, Guy and Leen, Jeff, *Kings of Cocaine*, Harper & Row, New York, 1990.

Inter-American Commission on Drug Policy, *Seizing Opportunities*, Institute of the Americas and the Center for Iberian and Latin American Studies at the University of California, San Diego, La Jolla, California, 1991.

Morales, Edmundo, *Cocaine: White gold rush in Peru*, The University of Arizona Press, Tucson, 1989.

Pacini, Deborah and Franquemont, Christine, (eds.), "Coca and Cocaine: Effects on people and policy in Latin America", Cultural Survival Report, No 23, Cultural Survival Inc., and

Latin American Studies Program, Cornell University, Cambridge, Massachusetts, 1986.

Panos Institute, *Beyond Law Enforcement: Narcotics and development*, Washington, DC, 1990.

Reid, Michael, "Una región amenazada por el narcotráfico", García-Sayán, (ed.), op. cit., pp133-169.

de Rementería, Ibán, "Sustitución de los Cultivos Ilegales de Coca: estrategia y plan de acción", *Boletin Comsion Andina de Juristas*, No 26, September 1990, pp17-30.
"La Sustitución de Cultivos Como Perspectiva", in García-Sayán, (ed.), op. cit., pp361-388.

Washington Office on Latin America, *Clear and Present Danger: The US military and the war on drugs in the Andes*, WOLA, Washington, DC, 1991.

Younger, Coletta, *The War in the Andes: The military role in US international drug policy*, WOLA, 1990.

Asia, opium and heroin

Crooker, Richard, "Forces of change in the Thailand opium zone", *The Geographical Review*, Vol 78, No 3, July 1988, pp242-256.

"The historical geography of opium production in the Southwest China region", proceedings of the Seventh International Symposium on Asian Studies, Asian Research Service, Hong Kong, 1985.

Lamar, Robert G. and Renard, Ronald D., "Opium crop substitution without fears or terror—the case of Northern Thailand, 1971-1989", prepared for the 1989 UNFDAC Regional Seminar on Replacement of Opium Poppy Cultivation.

Morante, Edith, (ed.), "Burma: in search of peace. A special report", *Cultural Survival Quarterly 13*, No 4, 1989, pp1- 41.

McCoy, Alfred, *The Politics of Heroin in South-east Asia*, Laurence Hill Books, Chicago, 1991.

McKinnon, John and Vienne, Bernard, (eds.), *Hill Tribes Today*, White Lotus-Orstom, Bangkok, 1989.

van der Meer, Cornelis L. J., "Problems and progress in crop replacement programmes in Burma, Pakistan and Thailand, 1972-1987: a review", manuscript.

Walker, Anthony, "The production and use of opium in the Northern Thai uplands: An introduction", *Contemporary Southeast Asia*, Vol 2, No 2, 1980, pp135-154.

Wiant, Jon A., "Narcotics in the Golden Triangle", *The Washington Quarterly*, Vol 8, No 4, Fall 1985, pp125-140.